Turbulence

Jenn & Jo

Merry Christmas!

I am hoping you are both enjoying your educational service.

See you next Summer!

Heamer or Tyle Hann

Turbulence

Leaders, Educators, and Students Responding to Rapid Change

Lyle Hamm

ROWMAN & LITTLEFIELD
Lanham • Boulder • New York • London

Published by Rowman & Littlefield
An imprint of The Rowman & Littlefield Publishing Group, Inc.
4501 Forbes Boulevard, Suite 200, Lanham, Maryland 20706
www.rowman.com

86-90 Paul Street, London EC2A 4NE

Copyright © 2021 by Lyle Hamm

All rights reserved. No part of this book may be reproduced in any form or by any electronic or mechanical means, including information storage and retrieval systems, without written permission from the publisher, except by a reviewer who may quote passages in a review.

British Library Cataloguing in Publication Information Available

Library of Congress Cataloging-in-Publication Data

Names: Hamm, Lyle, 1965- author.
Title: Turbulence : leaders, educators, and students responding to rapid
    change / Lyle Hamm.
Description: Lanham, Maryland : Rowman & Littlefield, 2021. |
    Includes bibliographical references.
Identifiers: LCCN 2021026560 (print) | LCCN 2021026561 (ebook) |
    ISBN 9781475849080 (cloth) | ISBN 9781475849097 (paperback) |
    ISBN 9781475849103 (ebook)
Subjects: LCSH: Educational change—Canada. | Educational
    change—United States. | Educational leadership—Canada. |
    Educational leadership—United States. | Community and school—Canada.
    | Community and school—United States.
Classification: LCC LA412 .H36 2021 (print) | LCC LA412 (ebook) |
    DDC 370.971—dc23
LC record available at https://lccn.loc.gov/2021026560
LC ebook record available at https://lccn.loc.gov/2021026561

∞™ The paper used in this publication meets the minimum requirements of American National Standard for Information Sciences—Permanence of Paper for Printed Library Materials, ANSI/NISO Z39.48-1992.

*To my mother Janice, and father Jerry, who gave
me life and my spirit for adventure.
To my brother Richard, and sister Alison for their strength and resilience.
To my grandparents Ernie, Eileen, Eugene, and Eva
for shaping my quest to learn and teach.
To my wife Lauren, daughter Delaina, and son-in-law
Mitch . . . your courage and strength are inspiring.
To Hope-Lynn, KayLee, William, Edouard, Axton, and Ember . . .
I encourage you to chase your dreams and work for peace.*

Contents

Foreword

The author of this book and I first met in 1994, when we both taught middle school in Southern Alberta. We have kept in touch throughout the years as we continue our journey as educators. My professional goal was to become an administrator and instructional leader after teaching as an elementary generalist, and high school specialist. Having actively sought out positions in diverse socioeconomic and geopolitical environments, I had the pleasure serving as an administrator and teacher in all twelve grades, and in both rural and urban communities. I have lived and taught school on an Indigenous reserve and on several Hutterian Brethren colonies. In these pandemic-shrouded days, I now teach students online.

Education is continually changing, evolving in a Darwinian process of survival and adaptation. New and improved theories for better learning, retention, skill-building, and critical thinking are produced continuously. Consequently, school leaders across the world are required to get better results on standardized tests.

Curriculum changes with politicians and geography. In Alberta, where I am writing from, there is a huge public outcry as the current government is proposing a new K–6 curriculum. The conservative right wing intends to include more American history, and very little about Canada's history of indigenous residential schools. This is aimed at countering the radical left dominant curriculum now in schools. Marlene Poitras, the regional chief of the Assembly of First Nations, argues "That is our history. The truth about our history, and especially in this time of reconciliation, does need to be told" (Bench, 2020). Teachers and administrators have little if any control or input into *what* is being taught, but perhaps we can influence *how* the curriculum is taught.

In the following chapters you will find a cogent and passionate discussion on the impact of an increasingly rapid rate of change in our society, and how the changes can be felt in the schools and classrooms in North America. Dr. Hamm argues that the upcoming generation is living in a drastically different world than the one we Boomers and Millennials were brought up in. Technology in the form of computers and smartphones have brought the internet, online gaming, Facebook, Twitter, Zoom, and social media of all descriptions into our society, homes, and, of course, into our classrooms. School districts are forced to create policy and programs to deal with technological issues that appear and disappear daily in a market accessible to our most vulnerable citizens, our children.

"School children are the largest untapped consumer market in our society; the public education system is the largest public enterprise still to be privatized" (Barlow and Robertson, 1994, p. 83). The world wants into our classrooms, craving access to that consumer demographic, and not all of the products are wholesome or beneficial for the children. Capitalism in our classrooms creates competition, teaching one worldview of economy results in an acceptance of a corporate identity, loyalty to brand, not to group, class, country, or union (Barlow and Robertson, 1994).

At the time of writing, we are in the midst of a global pandemic, in which isolation and loneliness are a part of life for both adults and children. Online learning has been dominating the news and students, parents, teachers, and school administrators have been scrambling to adapt to their new and ever-changing realities. Social unrest seems to be ubiquitous, civil wars continue in many places across the planet. We have recently witnessed democracy demonstrations in Myanmar, India, and Hong Kong, while anti-democracy riots occurred in Washington. Society is changing at a dizzying pace. How can schools possibly keep up?

Dr. Lyle Hamm has amazingly filtered all of this chaos and complexity into a collection of case studies, personal stories, field notes, and lived events that help explain, flesh out, elucidate, and bring to life the reality of teaching and learning in classrooms in 2021. It seems to make more sense when you can tell stories to illustrate the point that you are trying to make. Reading this book feels like a conversation we've had sitting around the campfire after a day on the water catching walleye. Yes, teaching, leading, and learning are complicated, complex, and difficult. But there is hope. There is always hope. Hope and resilience can be taught, and in these pages, we are given a road map toward a more collective and empowering environment in schools. The following chapters argue that it is necessary to build peace, empower collective leadership, utilize authentic, ethical, and inclusive strategies to create a school learning environment in which all students succeed.

There is a bit of wisdom, attributed to Albert Einstein: "If you always do what you always did, you will always get what you always got." So how do we change what we are doing to get the results that we are looking for? Read on intrepid learner, for the answers may reveal themselves. If not, at least you may begin another journey worthy of a story.

Joseph H. Buckler, M.Ed.
University of Lethbridge

REFERENCES

Barlow, M., & Robertson, H. J. (1994). *Class warfare: The assault on Canadian schools.* Toronto, ON: Key Porter Books.

Bench. A. (2020, October 21). UCP under fire for K–4 curriculum plans that suggest leaving out residential schools. Retrieved from https://globalnews.ca/news/7410812/alberta-curriculum-education-residential-schools/.

Preface

This book was written between January and December of 2020 when our world was terribly out of order. I did not intentionally wait for COVID-19 to strike and spread to begin writing. I believed the start of 2020 offered many reasons to be hopeful. After submitting my book proposal to Rowman & Littlefield in late 2018, I was fortunate to receive a two-year window to complete the project. I needed the time as I was teaching in 2019 and early 2020 and like most educators, I was running low on energy and did not feel I had the cognitive fuel and motivation to begin a book.

However, my university granted me a sabbatical year starting in July 2020. With uninterrupted time in my foreseeable future, my energy returned, and I knew I had an opportunity to submit a manuscript to the publisher by December 31, 2020.

But when COVID-19 began shutting down institutions, the book I had planned to write related to the day-to-day turbulence impacting schools and their inhabitants, took additional paths. I tried to stay as close to the writing plan as possible, but the societal changes, which at first were gradual, were then sudden and abrupt. Nearly everything stopped. Uncertainty became the norm. News related to the pandemic and how people should keep themselves safe changed daily, and at times, hourly. The whole world and many of its leaders lost all direction and went off-script. Many leaders became unrecognizable as they stepped in front of the media each day to provide their regions' updates.

As I situated myself into the writing process of late 2020 with a world on fire, my thinking always returned to the words of another contemporary writer who I had had the chance to listen to at an academic book launch in Ottawa in 2015. The writer gently reminded the educational leadership scholars who had gathered at the launch that it was important for them to write for the school leaders, teachers, and students they served through their service in higher education. He told everyone to write for the people in the daily trenches in K–12 schools and not just for themselves on their promotional journey through the academic ranks. I took his words to heart.

The year 2020 was to become the most turbulent year in recent times (Rath, 2020). As I buried myself into my writing at my off-grid cabin in central New Brunswick, the world was on hyper speed as it began to slow down. One paradoxical message after another were sent into multimodal transmission routes as the COVID-19 pandemic set its unknown course and trapped the entire world. Get people out of this country and that country quickly but start shutting down domestic and international land and air travel. Essential workers are required but they must have protection from potential viral infection; however, there is limited or no personal protective equipment at all to protect them. People do not have to wear face masks; people are encouraged to wear face masks; people now must wear face masks. The messaging changed as the contexts rapidly changed from day to day. There was no question that by the end of March 2020, the world was in severe turbulence and it continues as I write this preface in April 2021.

During the pandemic, things progressively got worse while they were already . . . worse. There were road and railway blockades in Canada stemming from historical oppression and grievances (Winter, 2020). There was a mass shooting in a Canadian province (Canadian Press, 2020). There were historical elections that would ultimately turn bloody and put democracy at risk (Tan et al., 2021). And the question for this book constantly plagued me as I continued to strategically commit my thoughts into text on each chapter based largely on what was occurring at that moment in time in 2020. *In a world that appears to be coming apart, how should educators in North America, that is, classroom teachers and school administrators who are in formal leadership positions, help their students understand and prepare for such troubling and turbulent times? What actions can and must they take to counter the confusion and complexity?*

As a former public school educator and administrator turned university teacher and researcher, I have hundreds of colleagues and graduate students all over Canada and around the world who I serve and collaborate with. I worried about those in the classroom who did not know what April 2020 would look like when they returned from the spring break. Most educators and students had to take their teaching and learning online in platforms that they had never encountered, or only employed superficially. I learned that teacher, school leader, student, and parental stress and anxiety were at all-time highs in the spring of 2020, and the summer of 2020 offered most of them little reprieve as they didn't know what their schools would like when they returned to them in September.

But humans are resilient. For the most part, educators are very flexible and even if many do not want to change their teaching strategies that much, they are still very good at adjusting their instructional methodologies when they must. You can never keep a teacher, school leader, or their students down that long. They bounce back stronger and become more resilient with time during the day-to-day complexities they face and that is what has happened in 2021. This book is for those teachers, school leaders, and students.

REFERENCES

Canadian Press. (2020, December 17) N.S. mass murderer killed after RCMP officers recognized him next to them at gas pump. *National Post Online.* Retrieved from https://nationalpost.com/news/canada/rcmp-officers-recognized-n-s-gunman-after-pulling-up-at-gas-pump-next-to-him

Rath, T. (2020, December 31). News story of the year: How COVID stole 2020. *The Fredericton Daily Gleaner,* A1–A2.

Tan, R., Jamison, P., Chason, R., Lang, M., & Cox, J. W. (2021, January 7). Chaos and violence as mob storms U.S. Capitol. *The Fredericton Daily Gleaner,* A1, A4.

Winter, J. (2020, February 13). The story from the Wet'suwet'en protest line. *National Observer Online.* Retrieved from https://www.nationalobserver.com/2020/02/13/news/story-wetsuweten-protest-line.

Acknowledgments

There are many people who have supported me throughout my educational career, and many more who have encouraged me to get this book written and closer to publication. Firstly, I would like to thank Mr. Tom Koerner from the education division of Rowman & Littlefield Publishers. Tom contacted me through email in May of 2015 after he had read my article in the *Principal Leadership* magazine. I am grateful for Tom's kindness, support, and encouragement for helping me make this story a reality. Tom, I hope to meet you in person one day.

I wish to thank Carlie Wall, managing editor at Rowman & Littlefield, for her encouragement and helping me keep my focus and stay close to my writing timelines. I am especially grateful for Carlie's support when COVID-19 hit the world and I required an extension to complete the first draft of *Turbulence*.

I received excellent feedback from several readers of my full manuscript. My sincere gratitude to Lyle Spencer, Joe Buckler, Ann DeVries, and Jerrold Hamm. Each of your responses to my writing was different and further challenged my thinking on later drafts. I really appreciate how each of you understood my thinking and made your own connections to the ideas. In one of the chapters, I infused an email conversation I had with my Uncle Lyle on the impact of technology on institutions. His wisdom profoundly made me reflect on what technology is out there and what is ACTUALLY out there and not quite ready for human interaction.

I would also like to thank my colleagues in the faculty of education at UNB. It is a real honor working with wonderful educators and leaders on a day-to-day basis. I look forward to the day when we are all together again in person.

Finally, I have been gifted throughout my life with wonderful friends, leaders, and mentors through education, sport, teaching, and coaching. There are far too many to mention here, but without their guidance, this book would never have been written.

Introduction

In 2021, it is difficult for me to be on the outside of public schools looking in, either as an educational researcher who briefly visits schools and talks to educators and students about leading, teaching, and learning, or simply as a social observer with an appetite for news of any kind related to schools. I was a teacher and school leader for twenty-two years from September 1991 until June of 2013. I then transitioned to the much slower paced environment of higher education where, for the past eight years, I teach mostly online courses to graduate students and hear the occasional sound of someone walking past my office. I often feel guilty. I have found this new academic life to be so unlike the accelerating day-to-day experiences I shared with my K–12 colleagues in Alberta. Planning for, teaching, leading, managing, coaching, mentoring, counseling, and just saving many, many students is hard work. In these six chapters, I have tried my best to capture and align many of my treasured experiences and significantly crucible educative moments with what I perceive to be some of the most pressing challenges educators and students encounter today. I did not try to write about everything. In a way, this book could be considered a snapshot of life inside schools the past twenty years, or a book that has attempted to humbly provide just a few snapshots.

Admittedly, as I wrote the chapters through 2020, I was challenged to stay with the script as it had been approved by Rowman & Littlefield. There was just too much going on that was important. As just one example, I submitted the first full draft of the book on January 4, 2021, and two days later, a violent siege occurred at the Capitol in Washington, D.C., as Congress was approving the 2020 election results (Tan et al., 2021). Again, I asked myself, how are educators talking about this significant event with long-lasting historical implications with their students? I just could not imagine. And yet, I had the unique opportunity to write about the turbulence and upheaval in society, that was most certainly impacting schools everywhere, in real time. I just kept typing.

I intentionally situate chapter one within the rapid changes and confusion of 2020 focusing on several events that placed the entire world on edge. The COVID-19 pandemic and the United States national election dominated the headlines in North America. A deadly tragedy in rural Nova Scotia in April shook Canada to its core just as its citizens were beginning their terrifying journey through the COVID-19 pandemic. Several additional topics are introduced that are developed with deeper considerations in the later chapters. The first case study of the book focuses on cell phone disruption in classrooms.

In the second chapter, I argue that collective leadership approaches that draw from inclusive, invitational, ethical, and social justice perspectives provide school leaders, educators, and students with useful cognitive tools for navigating the blurriness of leadership and learning in our current era. It is important for school leaders to clearly understand that they alone cannot lead a school in 2021 and beyond. They need leadership service from every corner of their learning community and this idea is developed in the chapter case study of Thom Gordon. School leaders and teachers must be *empowerment wielders* and challenge their students to develop their leadership skills in ways that they can. Further, the leadership that exists in communities within the school's catchment regions must be found and harnessed, particularly from the marginalized communities.

In chapter three, the development and proliferation of digital and communication technologies in schools is explored. The author describes how a blockbuster movie from 1983 foreshadowed the dominant role that computer technology was going to play in shaping some of the digital experiences of humans the following decades. The paradox of the internet and social media, playing out both goodness and evil in all its iterations and interconnections, is examined through school life stakeholders and day-to-day activities. Several questions in the activities section challenge readers to consider how the internet impacts their pedagogies and leadership.

Chapter four opens with an imaginative examination of a Grade 4 teacher's early morning drive and arrival in her diverse ethnocultural classroom at a Washington D.C., elementary school on November 4, 2020. Tensions continue to rise as she works to ameliorate the fears of her students while also addressing one student's curiosity about ocean plastics. Students are now part of and learning in a sanitized society in late 2020, if in fact they are able to attend school in their community. Students wear face masks and do their best to respond effectively on playgrounds to social distancing rules. Further, with immigration levels remaining high, teachers across North America face additional challenges in helping their newcomer students adjust to the culture and dominant discourses in their schools and communities.

The argument that runs through chapter four is that educators are not well positioned or prepared to respond to the needs of many newcomer children in their classrooms, particularly those children who have witnessed the butchery of war and civil unrest in the home countries they escaped from or left. Further, teachers are now having to respond pedagogically to the climate and environmental crisis confronting everyone on the planet. Amid the rising turbulence, the question is asked, how do teachers restore and nurture hopefulness in their students during these complex times?

Using poetry, chapter five opens with a story about how humans have created, confronted, endured, and survived turbulence and strife throughout history. More than ever, students attending schools need their educators to focus on stories of hope, resilience, and peace, and less on despair and destruction as the teacher in the opening excerpt learned. Curriculum choices matter in 2021. First and foremost, students need to be able to get along with their peers, understand the range of human diversity in their world, and work toward creating peace in their lives. This is a challenging task for young people and their teachers who lead them given the reality of social harming that plays out in society and now through social media and the internet. The chapter concludes with several strategies that educators, school leaders, and students may consider, to improve learning, teaching, leadership, and social inclusivity in their schools and communities.

The story that opens chapter six aligns all the major themes in the book and attempts to illustrate why peace is worth fighting for—why peace is desperately needed in our world. The author suggests that humanity is just one flashpoint away from a major social disruption in the world that may be difficult to recover from. If conflict continues at its rate and scale in the future, in real time or through digital platforms, then humans, those living today, and those not yet born, are in for a real struggle. In a moment in our history when all earthly and humanly constructed and shaped systems are in jeopardy, the COVID-19 pandemic brought humanity to its knees. It has given everyone an opportunity to pause. People must rethink some of their causes in life, or at least how they take their causes up in 2021, for our children to live together in peace and harmony. Being kind costs nothing; it is crucial that schools have peace plans or peace planning in place. It is also important to remember that students are the future. They need to be encouraged to be the agents of peace in a world of turbulence.

REFERENCES

Tan, R., Jamison, P., Chason, R., Lang, M., & Cox, J. W. (2021, January 7). Chaos and violence as mob storms U.S. Capitol. *The Fredericton Daily Gleaner,* A1, A4.

Chapter 1

Building Peace in a Complex and Turbulent Diverse World

"Shots fired!" echoes somewhere in North America.

The phrase has become synonymous with North American life in recent times. An opening chapter on building peace that is meant to engage and challenge leaders, educators, and students in schools as well as in the communities they serve, should not begin with such a phrase as it runs clearly counter in tone to the project. Reader, please be patient. The world is on fire and citizens everywhere find themselves in truly turbulent and dark times in 2020. There is currently no way to avoid, look beyond, or be dismissive about the challenges that confront everyone in society.

And the unpredictable times became worse for one province in Canada when a gunman went on an overnight and early morning killing spree in April 2020. Before he was shot and killed by police, twenty-two innocent people had lost their lives, their family members changed forever. Events such as these, like so many others the past few years, accelerate the heart rate. Reader, you must slow down. You must breathe.

As this book was written and completed, humans in every corner of the world are in the middle of a major coronavirus pandemic. It is the coronavirus disease 2019. The disease is commonly known as COVID-19. Each day people are becoming infected and many thousands are dying. Communities, provinces, and states shut down public and private organizations and businesses, reopen them, and later shut them down again. Many economic systems are at a standstill and political discourse wavers almost daily about the best ways to keep society open in order to keep people healthy. Politicians, medical officers, and community members debate rigorously on how to keep the darkness at bay.

A book about hope and peace must directly confront the current dark age if it has any chance for what Burns (1978) describes as transforming actions that humans—in the context of this book, that is school leaders, educators,

1

and their students, must consider as teaching and learning priorities that go beyond the mandated curriculum. Violent and dangerous events are sadly impacting teaching and learning in schools and communities throughout North America, creating fear and shaking the confidence of students and citizens.

Referencing the past twenty years, North Americans have experienced and witnessed events that at one time, only seemed possible in Hollywood action movies. Planes have plunged into and tumbled the great towers of New York City, a bomb destroyed a building in Oklahoma City, school and urban shootings are on the rise, and forests fires run rampant in both Canada and the United States. Land and oceans are becoming poisoned. The world is becoming increasing complex and turbulent and its impact reaches everyone. There is no denying these facts.

Further, humans seem trapped in a web of self-generated significance (Geertz, 1973) and it is digital, as millions of people are now perpetually fixated on the minute and hour to the latest tweets, Facebook and social media posts created by the political, social, and entertainment leaders and personalities in North America. This new norm raises an important question for this book: In a world that appears to be coming apart, how should educators in North America, that is, classroom teachers and school administrators who are in formal leadership positions, help their students understand and prepare for such troubling and turbulent times? What actions can and must they take to counter the confusion and complexity?

These are questions that are perplexing educators all over the planet as they seek meaning in the various conflicts they encounter daily through the print, digital online, and social media networks. In simpler terms, how must educators help their students understand what is going on in the world? More importantly, why is it important educators do so?

If you have begun to think that only a cynic would paint such a foreboding picture of our contemporary society at the opening of a book on leadership and education, reader, you are reminded to be patient once again. It is difficult writing this book in 2020 as there is no clear leadership now in the United States (as of December 31, 2020), and it seems to be hanging on hinges in Canada. Leadership is being called into question everywhere. For instance, in Canada, several politicians have been caught traveling abroad during the COVID-19 pandemic, when they insisted that all Canadians stay home over the holidays. Hypocrisy seems to be at an all-time high with many leaders. One wonders, "Do I follow, or go my own way?"

Leading is difficult and this author understands that any criticism of leadership at any level must align with the leadership the said critic has contributed to roles in their life. That is, if you have not been in a leadership position or role, you might not know what you are really talking about or criticizing.

Leading is hard work. Leading in these times of 2020 is nearly impossible. But the world needs leaders. Pivot time. Fast forward to November 2020.

THE WORLD WATCHES AN ELECTION

So, in the United States, the election happened, one president lost, and one president-elect is preparing to take office. No one knows for sure what will happen in the next several months or year. Democracy is under attack and teachers and students are grappling with this phenomenon. Through all of this and what may come out of it, the reader must be assured that this book will be first and foremost about hope, possibility, and human connection. Traditional leadership theories do not seem to be working in 2020. New theories and ways of thinking and seeing the world must emerge to suggest and provide strategies for educators. Further, educators must be flexible in adapting their own learning and teaching protocols to guide them in charting their work with children in their schools and communities. All that said, it is important to identify the problem(s) before any solution(s) can be designed. And our current social realities suggest that the world is becoming increasingly turbulent, tumultuous, troublesome, and nearly impossible to comprehend. Take for instance what happened in the province of Nova Scotia, Canada, on April 18 and 19, 2020.

PERPETRATOR DRESSED AS A POLICEMAN

The world woke up on April 19, 2020, to learn that there was a gunman on the loose in rural Nova Scotia, a province on the east coast of Canada. The province is home to nearly one million Atlantic Canadian citizens. The province is surrounded by ocean with its only land border connected to its neighboring province of New Brunswick. As details slowly emerged the following week and months, news addicts gradually learned the extent of the gunman's carnage.

The conflict had started as a domestic dispute and then spilled into adjacent properties and laneways. By midnight, thirteen people lay dead. The suspect was obsessed with policing and had purchased, over the course of several years, four police cruisers. Along with his heavy arsenal of weapons, he had a police uniform. In his professional life, he was a denturist. On this night and early morning, he would become Canada's most wanted criminal.

The police arrived at the scene along with several ambulances and health care workers and with only one road in and out of the community, they believed they had the suspect cornered within the parameters of multiple crime scenes he had created. Along with the victims, the first responders found several homes and vehicles burning, including two unmarked former police vehicles. A third vehicle was parked in a nearby city where the suspect lived. What the police did not know at that time was that there was a fourth car, completely painted to look like a modern police vehicle. Thinking that they had the suspect cornered, they learned the following morning that he had somehow eluded them and drove away from the crime scene across a field to continue his human slaughter.

Some of the victims were known to the suspect; some were not. He used his disguise to pull people over and shoot them in the car or as they were walking along the road in their community. At 11:26 a.m. on April 19, the suspect stopped at a gas station and was engaged by two plainclothes officers driving an unmarked police vehicle who were on their way to support the investigation. The suspect was killed.

This event occurred at a time when the coronavirus pandemic was near its first peak in Nova Scotia, Canada, and the rest of the world. Citizens were already on edge while isolated in their homes, glued to their televisions and electronic devices, wondering when life could ever return to the normal routines they knew prior to the worldwide outbreak of the disease.

There is no going back now, and it is important to make that clear at the front of this book. Reader, there is no going back. There is no way to bring the victims of the Nova Scotia massacre back, to effectively heal all the people who lost loved ones and friends in the shootings, to soothe the mass hysteria pervasive in every mind that is wondering, "Could that have been me?" The answer is yes. It could have been. But again, the reader is invited to return to the question for this book, slightly altered to shake away passive slumber.

If the world seems or is blatantly on the verge of coming apart due to global pandemics (the current one and in the future), mass shootings (pick your country), economic meltdown and despair, environmental damage, social unrest everywhere, and educational shutdown, how should educators help their students understand and prepare for such troubling and turbulent times? It has been a question plaguing this writer for nearly twenty years of his educational and community service. It is a question that is making this book so difficult to write. The context changes weekly, daily, hourly, and minute by minute. The context is difficult to capture and if captured, it seems to remain in the mind for a fleeting moment. Then the context changes again.

But readers, you cannot run and hide from any of the named complexities. This is especially true for educators and leaders in schools whose students rely upon. They need competent adults and educators in their lives to construct and lead their lessons effectively, and not shelter, run from, nor hide from the current complex moments in our history.

In fact, it would be a difficult task for anyone who follows the news—both real and perceived—on the multiple platforms that it is now delivered to the masses of information consumers—to refute the fact that "something is rotten in the state" of our world and it needs fixing (Shakespeare in Evans, 1974). Solutions of any substance and sustainable qualities do not happen quickly in this age where millions of media consumers draw sustenance from misery, conflict, and the time they commit to building their online social presence.

There is growing apathy in the public toward crucial world events and it must be confronted, countered, and conquered. To understand this, one simply must scroll through the comments sections that lay below the news stories published online. By compounding these conflicts and social realities with the steady diet of racism, discrimination, and intolerance that is being perpetually generated from all corners of our society, the work of educators in 2020 seems insurmountable. But that just gives an abundance of reasons for a book like this.

Teaching and leading in these rapidly changing times is not impossible and insurmountable. And framing the title with turbulence has not be the first time an author has done so the past twenty years (Goddard, 2000; Patterson, Goens, and Reed, 2009). The world is turbulent, tumultuous, and complex. More than ever, educators must perceive their work and service for the betterment of human beings in a healthy and sustainable world. Educators must reset their own educational compasses to assist them in navigating and finding solutions to the conflicts that confront them daily. The turbulence and complexity must be used as fuel for the cognitive engines of school leaders, educators, and their students. If it should be perceived otherwise, it may burn educators and students to the ground.

The key messages in this book will challenge readers to act on the local and global events that matter to them. They can take actions that will have a positive impact on the lives of the students they lead and even on the communities in which they serve. Education is fraught with challenge and adversity, but it is still very much about hope, peace, and opportunity for human growth, regardless of what is occurring in the world.

Educators and school leaders who lead children or guide the teachers who serve children cannot stray from this universal mandate or calling. Simply put, now more than ever, our society needs educators and student leaders, and they must be humans with caring hearts, courage, and stamina who know that by answering the call of the classroom and of their society, they will forever be on the front lines of combating social ills.

Educators must possess a speculative imagination (Baillie; introduction in Hegel, 2003, p. xv) much like Miguel Cervantes had and portrayed through his errant knight, Don Quixote, who chased evil visions in his mind to right a world of wrongs. The tragic hero in the classic tale imagined what people could become and what his social world could be like (Cervantes, [1605 and 1615] 1986). He was crazy, yes. But he was filled with a vision of hope and his hope became a positive contagion. And for this world, we need a positive contagion.

LIVING IN REAL TIME

For peace to occur and for hope to germinate and take root in our society, classrooms, and communities, whatever they will look like after the COVID pandemic, people have to come together, talk together, and stay connected with each other, in real time. And it is *real time* that is not simply *online time.* Real time as posited here is the flesh and blood real time, where the body gestures that individuals convey in communicating with other humans are as important as the words that are spoken with them. And people must come out from behind their cell phones and tablets that serve as their shield and be together again in their community social spaces more than they are online. Is this a bold claim or suggestion? The author will stand by it.

People need to reconnect much more effectively as they once did just ten years or so ago, when cell phones, laptops, and tablets did not define them. The smart technology was certainly not part of their identity formation as it has become today. Have you heard about the current phenomenon behind obtaining the perfect selfie? Understandably, pontificating such as this requires additional unpacking. So, reader, what does this mean? Well, it means two more things that this introductory chapter will introduce with extrapolation in the following chapters—social media over usage and increasing immigration.

SOCIAL MEDIA DISCONNECTIONS

Okay, reader, go outside where you are right now. That is, if you are not in a present lockdown somewhere in the world. If you are, put your mask on. By the time this book is published, there is hope that people will be outside again, and life will be near normal. Are you reading this book in a small community in Alberta or Manitoba? Or are you in a medium-sized city in northern California or Maine? Or are you strolling a beach in the hamlets, towns, and cities on the eastern or western coastlines of Canada or the United States? Wherever you are, it does not really matter. The burning question is: besides the situations, environments, and beautiful natural landscapes you might be looking over, are you interacting with and/or paying attention to the social interactions of the people around you? What are they doing? What are they talking about? What are they looking at?

Chances are, if you are near several people or better yet, in a crowd of people and your own head is up (This is recommended more than ever in 2020 as the first part of this chapter laid out), and your senses are doing what they are supposed to—that is, they are helping you see, smell, and even feel your way through your environment. You are in control of your own body movements in space by being aware of your surroundings so you can interact with them, take in information, and protect yourself. There just might be several people with their heads down and fingers scrolling on their smartphone. Is this true? Is this really being smart?

Have You Ever Experienced This?

Here is a modern image that, in a modest academic view, deserves case study status in leadership courses that cover topics on effective communication. Enter a busy restaurant (with this book to read of course) and order a meal and continue reading this section of chapter one but keep your cell phone in your purse or pocket lest you be called a hypocrite. Mind you, it is getting increasingly difficult for many people in the modern digital world to not be contaminated with the hypocrisy that they also purchase (perhaps unknowingly) along with their cell phone.

Do not worry about that just yet. Focus on this image. Is there a table nearby with several family members or friends gathered? If so, is one, or several of them, or all of them looking at their screens? Keep watching them. How long does it take until one breaks the code of digital silence at the restaurant table? Oh, it is so hard to not be called out on this one, because everyone who owns a cell phone does this (as does this author).

The imagery presented above is simply meant to stir your attentions and help you become aware of the new normal social behavior if you have not already. Multiple studies may be referenced at this point to confirm this new and evolving social reality, but it is not necessary. Those writers know who they are. And to be sure, this early inquiry in this book is not intended to be or become an attack on cell phone communication. And further, it is not meant to be a verbal assault on the level of screen engagement citizens around the world are having with their friends, family members, and colleagues at work. Staying connected any way you can in a pandemic is vital to mental health.

Additionally, there is an absence of malice toward people who choose their battles with strangers and digital nemeses on their social media platforms like Facebook, Twitter, or the latest digital tool that connect people who are walking, standing, sitting, or even lying down at great distances from each other. Truly, it is amazing that such communication can be realized in our current age. Humans in 2020 are fortunate to have such tools at hand, especially in 2020 during a pandemic. Electronic devices have kept people in contact with each other. They are great in many ways. But in many ways, they are not that great. That is the first paradox of the book. Smartphones and social media are great and not that great.

There are unfortunate additional realities, that people may wish to consider as they align themselves with the advancing communication technologies—realities that are becoming darkly ubiquitous in our society. People who are walking around in small and large communities with their heads down and eyes and attention fixed to their small screens on their smartphones are at risk for injury.

Not only are they unable to be aware of passing vehicles speeding rapidly by them on roads, sidewalks, and at crosswalks; worse yet, there are predatory individuals or even groups of people who may be ready to pounce on them to take criminal advantage of persons-unaware. Like the shooter did in Nova Scotia. What about our youth who are often bullying and taking criminal advantage of their peers in schools and from the privacy of their homes simply because they can do so through their digital technologies?

Further, it is hard not to speculate that digitally fixated people are slowly going blind when you observe people squinting hard to read their text messages. The world will receive an abundance of research in the future to confirm or challenge this. No doubt the large tech corporations will dispute such research. That game of cat and mouse is always present in our mass-producing, consumer-based world. And that is a problem too, shortly to be addressed.

But clearly, people constantly on their smartphones are at serious risk in socially disengaging with their natural or human-constructed environments. In signing up for this new social arrangement (one needs a phone contract, right?), people are missing seconds, minutes, and hours of their lives. When you add that time up, addicted cell phone users are losing days of their lives while strolling toward their destination with a continuous partial attention (Rose, 2010) to several things and nothing all at once.

In the mid-1990s, this behavior was termed "multitasking" and seemed to elevate people in their working lives. But it really did not. Multitasking made people more anxious, depressed, and ultimately ineffective in their jobs. Society is witnessing the effects of that in today's world with the rise in diagnosed anxiety diseases. For those individuals who did master the art of multitasking, their reward was even more work. "If you want something done, give it to the busiest person!"

But like everything that begins innocently, multitasking has given way to digital addiction and in many cases, despair. Sadly, many people in our modern world are reaching tipping points where they can no longer discern the very realities that they encounter each day. Instead, while being constantly imprisoned by their smart devices, laptops, and computers, they are missing the important "moments on the way" to wherever they may be going. Does it mean anything?

Does it mean that they are missing an opportunity to see something, or meet someone, or catch a scent of something that could invite them to discover or rediscover something that might lead them to something that is very much more important than the messaging that they are creating, sending, and waiting for reply in the online digital world? That was an intentionally long sentence because that is how the world races with this technology. People are on technology all the time and looking for ways to break free of the constraints. Why are many humans seemingly not interested in the "moments on the way?" Sadly, our society appears to be accepting behaviors that even a few years ago would have been socially unacceptable.

CASE STUDY: STEALING LEARNING TIME FROM STUDENTS

University teachers, researchers, and public educators who share in similar human-service experiences and environments share stories of adult students in their classrooms who cannot leave their cell phones alone for the length of a class lecture. Think about that. University courses generally run between one hour and three hours each face-to-face meeting. Three-hour courses typically provide students a break at the halfway point in the class.

An emergent theme in discussions between university teachers leading undergraduate and graduate courses is that their students are constantly checking their phones, or their fingers are tapping it while it lay close by. Simply, students are now having to work harder to pay attention to the conversations in the class because their minds are on their phone in front of them. It is as if their smart devices on the table in front of them serve as a type of social compass for them in their classes and during their meetings. Without that phone, many people seem terribly lost—even vulnerable.

Now the reader might imagine that these behaviors are relegated to the newer university students who have just graduated from high school and are enjoying their first year of independence away from their homes and communities where they grew up. After all, it might be easy to forgive such North American students, as they are often labeled the "digital natives" (Kivunja, 2014). This generation has been educated the past two decades with the internet, classroom computers and laptops, fixed or movable SMART Boards and wireless connections that are increasingly available in their schools, shopping malls, or favorite teenage hangout.

It is amazing to observe several young adults who fit this stereotype sitting in a restaurant within arm's length of their friends with their heads down and scrolling their phones. They are not talking with each other as they once did a decade ago within the same context, and when their food arrives, they carry on, fixated to their phones, eat their meals and occasionally verbally engage one of their peers at their table as was earlier described. Again, this is not meant to be judgment; they are just observations and analytical reflective wonderings of where this may all be going. It is something very important to wonder about in 2020 because it is impacting teaching and leadership as later chapters will describe and examine.

Okay, but it is also important not to pick on our young adults (the 15–25-year-olds) for their digital behaviors in public and employment spaces. Unfortunately, the behavior is becoming more present among classroom teachers and leaders in the educational world, where people are paid to teach and provide leadership. Here is another fictional-based-on-substantial fact-case study to consider. Juxtaposing the real with the fiction in the next few lines, paints a picture of where the technology may be taking a wrong turn for our learning society and in schools, if in fact some serious discussions do not take place about this type of digital pedagogy being utilized in the educational service of North American school-aged children.

"Miss, YOU are ALWAYS on your Phone!"

A superintendent walked into a middle school classroom to observe and assess the pedagogical and professional behaviors of a first-year teacher. Now reader, if you have had the opportunity to work with middle school students (aged anywhere from 10–15 years old depending on how each school district classifies these children), you will clearly understand that young adolescents love drama and excitement, and they enjoy creating and participating in it whenever they can. As an aside, traditional educators trapped in 2020, it is also important to note that most of them do not like sitting in hard desks organized in long rows either.

Chalk it up to the stage of their physical, psychological, and emotional development that they are progressing through in early teenage years if you like, but if you have classroom and leadership experience working with young teenagers, you will know that their restlessness, their moral compass, and their sense of social justice often run parallel to the other until a moment surfaces where they all intersect and collide with brutality.

The supervision scene continues, and the young teacher carries on teaching a lesson at the front of the classroom. Many students, noticing the superintendent, are keen to discover how this situation might turn out. The usual fart or burp generally interrupts the summative assessment protocol with a giggle here and there. These adolescent actions are generally the benign stuff that everyone lives through during teacher observation and the feedback session. The teacher, exuding an already shaky level of confidence on this day, acknowledged her senior colleague and began to stretch the lesson on its carefully constructed pathway.

Within a few seconds, the young teacher's cell phone beeped on the side of her hip where it was firmly lodged in Clint Eastwood style in its leather case. It was a subtle and contemporary noticeable noise and would not have caused major disruption if it happened anywhere but here in this moment of assessment. Alas, there is a lot at stake here, most notably the young teacher's ability to feed, clothe, and shelter herself with the income she receives as part of the social contract in her service for these middle school students.

All eyes in the room averted to the phone (including the teacher's), then to the teacher, and then to the superintendent, who did not know if he should note the moment or carry on. After all, he was a thirty-year veteran with many complex experiences to his credit. However, until recently, the digital age was something he had never had to respond to in his previous service. So, with a kind heart, he kept his head down and smiled forgivingly. Besides, he wanted the young teacher to do well and hoped that his presence in the social environment did not increase the level of disruption and anxiety for the pedagogue and her students. He sincerely did not wish to function as a power impediment in the progress of her lesson.

The lesson continued for two minutes and things seemed to settle down and stay as teacher-planned. In fact, the teacher was considered a strong young pedagogue by her school principal and she got back into her groove. Then her phone beeped again. This time, the teacher could not avoid addressing the distraction and looked to her boss and said, "I am really sorry. I forgot to shut off my phone before the lesson."

The superintendent politely nodded his forgiveness again. However, that did not stop several students from gasping at the teacher's comment. Then the final blow was delivered on the lesson as one young lady in the middle of the classroom had the courage to say rather bluntly, as middle school students might, "Miss, YOU are ALWAYS on your phone when you are teaching us!" And then there was real-time drama.

NEW REALITY IN THE DIGITAL AGE?

Is this the new reality for North American classrooms and for our educational world in general? Are cell phone and smart devices productive learning technologies that are so important in a student's learning that every teacher always needs them at hand in the service of their students? The future may provide some illumination on this matter. People are arguing and debating this question through multiple platforms and yes, both sides are providing reasonable and interesting responses.

On one side, there is no question that with the increase in school violence across North America and around the world, the cell phone is a very useful tool for instant communication between educators, between school leaders and law enforcement officers, and between students and their parents if they find themselves locked down in their classrooms with a violent person on the landscape.

Still others suggest that educators who are addicted to their phones, like the young teacher in the case study above, are stealing time away from students and their learning. The most vulnerable students in our society—those who struggle with reading, basic math, and with their social and emotional skill development are the students who need their teachers to be on their game each class, each day, and each week. They deserve well-constructed and highly engaging educational service so that they can attain the educational goods and advantages that they need so they can exist productively and healthy in their futures.

Any way you slice this reality, it is complicated and complex and contributes to the turbulence that educators and leaders face in their jobs, and students face in their learning. There will be additional examination on this matter in a later chapter.

There is no way that one book can address all the challenges and conundrums that school leaders, educators, and their students are confronting in this modern era. And this book will not attempt to do that. The last few years, there have been several authors who have made their contributions to this conversation and perhaps that is all this writer, in crafting this book, will do. That is, he will add to and illuminate another part of the conversation at this crucial moment in our collective history in the conundrum year of 2020.

Researchers and educators in the field are positioned well to provide observations, but those observations will often be confined to the contexts that they evolved from. The following section is another North American context that is becoming more accessible to learn about through our print, television, and digital social medias.

"Where Are You From?"

A second observation for this book is related to the four words in the subheading that form the question that often surfaces when people, or groups of people, meet each other for the first time. Certainly, the question might take a moment or two to arise in a conversation, but the question covers multiple social environments across North America. One cannot avoid the question when watching or reading news about the increasing migration of populations around the world. Face it, immigration and the politics and views attached to the social phenomenon are constantly generating stereotyping, mistrust, and fear in our social world.

When people from dominant cultures in North America find themselves with individuals who do not share similar Eurocentric ethnic and ethnocultural backgrounds as they do, or similar religious affiliations or even sexual orientations, the question generally sneaks into the conversation and always seems to matter. Why? Is it because people notice difference? They notice the color of a person's skin; they notice a turban, or a hijab being worn, they notice subtle body movements and gestures that identifies a person as different from them.

This may all be fine, and construct a reasonable pathway to follow in the conversation, but why does it seem so important for one human being to question another on things unfamiliar to them in a social situation that might not warrant the question? Most importantly, why does the question often arrive at the front of the conversation?

For instance, after getting to know a person from the country of Nigeria for some time (I chose Nigeria because I have a good friend from there and we have had this conversation), it might seem prudent and educationally valuable for both participants to form their relationship further through discussing the common social events, issues, and societal challenges that shape both their nations. Topics such as racism, discrimination, the types of governments in power, and even how to understand the rules of a hockey game and how the rules work to regulate a teams' actions on the ice, might seem like logical conversational pathways to follow in dialogue after a relationship has been established.

The problem in our contemporary North American society it seems is that people jump to the awkward questions first, like, "Where are you from? Why are you here? What are you doing for work? Are you staying long?" By setting such inquiries, the questions then place strains on relationship-building long afterward through the mistrust that the questions might give rise to. This person has dark skin, this person's skin is even darker, and this person's skin color is lighter than both and yet, it is not completely white as many might suggest or even wish it to be. My gosh, how the color of a person's outer skin layers has caused such turbulence for generations in our society. Color is a social construct invented in the minds of humans and used to classify, organize, and unfortunately oppress and marginalize.

Again, this line of thinking is not meant to be anything more than educative and imaginative speculation (Baillie in Hegel, 2003). If as a society we are unable to get past the discrimination and hatred that color, culture, and religion stir up, then as a society, we are truly in for a rough ride. Some have said the next decade could be worse than what society is currently living through (Wood, 2020).

There may be no diligent argument now to ameliorate the anger and distrust that so many people feel because of something as beautiful as the color of a human being's skin. Schools in North America may very well be the only environment left where teachers, leaders, and children have a chance to craft a new narrative about diversity and color. After all, it is only through the children, what they are taught, what they learn and how it shapes their social behaviors that our society is going to stand a fighting chance to survive in the future. But it is still too early in this thinking in the book to turn to that. That will be for another chapter.

PEOPLE ARE ARRIVING IN NORTH AMERICA WITH NO PLACE LEFT TO GO

Canada and the United States boast huge geographical regions. In recent years, both countries have seen rising numbers of asylum seekers, immigrants, refugees escaping war zones, and temporary foreign workers entering their countries—most legally, but some illegally. Digital, print, and television newscasts suggest that both countries are rapidly exhausting their financial and social resources for settling newcomers in their respective societies.

When Donald Trump became the president of the United States, thousands of people fled that country by weathering dangerous winter conditions to walk across the Canadian/U.S. borders of Manitoba and Quebec simply for a chance to remain in North America. Elsewhere in the world, one reporter suggested that "the migration crisis will shatter Europe" (Wente, 2018) and the tolerance level of many Americans and Canadians are being challenged with the continuous surge of newcomers to their countries.

Regardless of how you view these contemporary events, the social reality is that for many communities across North America—children who are escaping into both countries with their parents will one day arrive at a school in Canada and the United States. Add to this complexity the fact that in both countries, intolerance of immigrants is growing at alarming rates. According to Egbo (2019), "Xenophobia, particularly toward new immigrants, is becoming prevalent in Western societies as a consequence of unprecedented population shifts . . . These tensions can easily spill into schools, and educators must be alert to the early warning signs of such conflicts among their students" (p. 13). Teachers in both countries and across the world must be, or commit to become, effectively prepared and educated to respond to their complex needs.

BUILDING PEACE THROUGH STORYTELLING

For many educators in Canada and the United States, to become a life-long learner or "scholar teacher" in a formal sense through attending university classes in face-to-face, on-campus programs, often takes a monumental commitment due to North American geography. In the Canadian context, it is a large country that spans ten provinces and three territories, and it is geographically located above the United States of America, which is, in geographical territory, almost as large as Canada.

For some additional context for the international readers of this book, the distance between Victoria, the capital city of the most western province, British Columbia, and St. John's Newfoundland on Canada's furthest east coast is over seven thousand kilometers. In total, from west to east and north to south, Canada covers almost ten million square kilometers, which translates into nearly four million square miles.

And though Canada has more land space than our southern U.S. neighbors, it only has one-tenth of its population, which aside from the frigid northern temperatures and isolated location on the planet, might then seem like a safe destination country to relocate your family to if you have been forced out of your own country by war, famine, or from oppressive living conditions and governing policies. In fact, there is a lot of land in Canada that has still not seen the footprints of humans.

The North American geographical reality has implications for educators, especially for those who aspire to break through and challenge their own ethnocentric worldviews and escape the bonds of regional attitudes. In graduate education programs, like the one in the Faculty of Education at the University of New Brunswick in Fredericton, New Brunswick (and undoubtedly elsewhere), faculty and sessional instructors are supporting educators from across Canada and even from around the world in rigorous, meaningful, and collegial online graduate programs.

This is not one author's attempt to convince readers of the benefits of completing a master's degree or a principal preparation program; it is an attempt to describe to readers how university and K–12 educators from across a large country like Canada, are working professionally and collaboratively to understand the complexities of their communities, schools, and classrooms. And for many, this learning is taking place right from their own offices and homes.

When they are faced with the question: "*What are the most complex educational and societal challenges you are facing in your schools and communities right now?*" students in online graduate programs have the time to think through the question before they must provide a response for their colleagues. They have a great deal of academic satisfaction unpacking and placing their ideas together in online discussion forums and then the group dialoguing subsequently yields a lot of rich information to consider and analyze over the week and duration during the course.

In fact, by providing questions like this one, the activity generates multiple themes that educators across North America are resonating with in their own schools and communities. Further, guiding questions allow them to highlight their own concerns as important entry points for course discussions, student reflection, and culminating papers and projects on their service in their schools and communities. In fact, it is inspiring how such a simple activity can ignite course discussions that motivate students to reflect on possibilities for change in themselves and within their educational organizations. Many of them then take their work into their communities.

By choosing to describe this learning context and present the guiding question and scenarios above as the opening frames for this book positions the idea that Canada and the United States are continuously evolving countries in the new millennium, given the complex and turbulent conditions each country is facing in 2020, and especially during a global pandemic. Both countries are rich in cultural, religious, and linguistic diversity dating back to the First Nations Peoples who occupied the vast lands and environments prior to the arrival of Europeans in the early 16th and 17th centuries.

They are countries with still vast abundant natural resources, clean air, and open space and because of these facts, they are countries that arguably boast opportunities for everyone who choose to live there and raise their families during these times of rapid change, social uncertainty, and through the turbulence that schools and communities across our nations are confronting. American educator and researcher William Greenfield (1993) noted a while ago that,

> As the populations served by public schools become increasingly diverse, school administrators must become proactive in creating environments for students, teachers, and parents that are supportive and inclusive of differences and that are responsive to the rapidly changing social contexts within which schools must operate. (p. 267)

Greenfield's insights are very important for educators and policymakers everywhere. Disease, conflict, and war in this new millennium has a long reach and its grasp is not loosening on the many countries in the world that are embroiled in their own difficulties. Further, countries that claim to be at peace, like Canada and the United States, are now finding thousands upon thousands of people entering their nations in various legal and illegal ways to either escape from the atrocities occurring in their homelands or the threat of being sent back there. Canada and the United States are two such countries that refugees, new immigrants, and international students and their families are looking to for support and for a fresh start in their lives.

THE IMPORTANCE OF STORIES FOR UNDERSTANDING OUR TURBULENT SOCIETY

American Aboriginal author Thomas King has said (2003), "The truth about stories is that that's all we are" (p. 2). If it is the moral objective of educators, students, community leaders, and governments to create peace and harmony within their institutions and public spaces (and it may not be a priority among many), then they will have to be committed at the core educational level to invite and bring the diverse populations in their communities throughout North America together. This is certainly not a new thought.

However, with the world on fire, racism, hatred, and discrimination is rampant, and the threat of and acts of violence have characterized some of the most highlighted news events of the past years, and specifically in 2020. What is often missing from the daily news cycles are the stories of hope, peace, and community-building that ultimately connect people together. Or these stories are just hard to find.

Paulo Freire (1970) suggests that storytelling is a dialogical learning experience and people who share stories may become bonded and sealed together in relationship through a reciprocal process. One story leads to another to form the dialogical connection between storyteller and listener and then loop back the other way. If storytelling becomes political, as is often the case in North America, and it flows in only one direction, an imbalanced and incomplete picture is formed in the mindsets of North Americans creating fertile soil for social hostility (Robertson, 2005). North Americans need the whole story, and they need to get back to storytelling at the school and community level, especially given the social climate in our current society.

As diligent as transforming educators and school leaders may be working to build safe classrooms and schools in North America, it is becoming more evident each year that divisions in our society are growing and growing at alarming rates. Given the current social climate and unrest in our society, if the people you are trying to bring together to learn about each other do not trust one another enough to have a dialogically reciprocal conversation without judgment—and are quite suspicious of the dearly important cultural and linguistic symbols and worldviews that guide each other and their families along their life trajectories—then humanity, as mentioned early, is surely in for a rocky ride in the next few years.

Further, if you are a steady consumer of current news affairs, you might argue favorably with this author that in 2020, we need positive stories more than ever. As Dylan Wiliam once said, "We are preparing our students for a world we cannot yet begin to comprehend" (Personal Communication, October 2011). By that statement, one must wonder what the next few years might bring to educators and what skills, abilities, and dispositions they need to help students develop what they will need to thrive beyond 2020.

When one considers the current national and global realities in North America that is characterized by competition in its many iterations and violence at levels that might make even Superman and Wonder Woman stay home, this writer finds solace in Parker Palmer's view (2016) that we need stories. But we need to

> stop throwing ideologies at each other and start telling stories of our own life. What do we love? What do we fear? It turns out we love a lot of the same things; we fear a lot of the same things. And if we keep it on the story-telling level we can eventually come to a place of human convergence where we may not change each other's minds but we will be reminded that in the long run, it's much more important to be in the right relationship than it is to be right and that to me is a hopeful fact. (interview with CBC *Tapestry* host, Mary Hynes, April, 2016)

This chapter will close with a story that Lisa Delpit (2006) learned when she was working with Arapaho children in the United States. Pius Moss, an Arapaho elder, helped the Western-educated researcher to understand the story writing and storytelling of his peoples' children. The researcher asked Pius why the Arapaho students wrote stories that she was unfamiliar with and that went against the writing norms and lessons she had been educated in and subsequently taught in her classes. In her words, the stories from the Arapaho children, "just ambled along with no definite start or finish, no climaxes, or conclusions" (Delpit, 2006, p. 61). Pius Moss explained that,

> Arapaho stories are not written down, they're told in what we might call serial form, continued night after night. A "good story is one that lasts seven nights . . . there is no ending to life, and stories are about Arapaho life, so there is no need for a conclusion." (Delpit, 2006, p. 61)

At the end of the day, it is important for educators to work toward peace in their classrooms, schools, and communities and through the following chapters, a framework will be advanced by examining the complex and turbulent world, that may further support educators and their students in their transformative work (Shields, 2018). Amid all the conflict that greets viewers, listeners, and smart device scrollers each morning when they wake up, it is important to remain hopeful and optimistic and visualize a shared world that is still full of beauty and wonder.

Peace is worth fighting for as Desmond Doss argued when challenged by the paradox of being a soldier without a rifle during World War II. "With the world so set on tearing itself apart, it doesn't seem so bad to me to want to put a little bit of it back together" (Gibson, 2016). Like Don Quixote in the late Middle Ages and Pius Moss in our modern age, Doss worked hard at creating a new narrative, a new story, to restore hope, build peace, and construct a new pathway for humans to follow. Our world needs dreamers and visionaries more than ever to get past 2020.

CHAPTER 1 ACTIVITY AND QUESTIONS

1. Do a jigsaw or world café activity. Here are some guiding questions you might consider: What are the most complex educational and societal challenges you are facing in your schools and communities right now? What are the current complexities in our world, community, and school? What are the social issues that matter to you that need to be addressed? How will you address them?
2. Does your cell phone own you? Can you go twenty-four hours without using it? Explain.
3. What is your vision of the leadership, post–COVID-19?

REFERENCES

Burns, J. M. (1978). *Leadership.* New York: Harper and Row Publishers.

Cervantes Saavedra, Miguel de. [1605, 1615] (1986). *The adventures of don quixote de la mancha.* New York: Farrar, Straus and Giroux.

Delpit, L. (2006). *Other people's children: Cultural conflict in the classroom.* New York: The New Press.

Egbo, B. (2019). *Teaching for diversity in Canadian schools (Second edition).* Toronto: Pearson.

Freire, P. (1970). *Pedagogy of the oppressed.* New York: Continuum.

Geertz, C. (1973). *The interpretation of cultures.* New York: Basic Books.

Gibson, M. (2016). *Hacksaw ridge* [Film]. Summit Entertainment.

Greenfield, W. D. (1993). Articulating values and ethics in administrator preparation. In C. Capper (Ed.), *Educational administration in a pluralistic society*, pp. 267–287. Albany: SUNY Press.

Goddard, J. T. (2000). Teaching in turbulent times: Teacher's perceptions of the effects of external factors on their professional lives. *Alberta journal of educational research, 46*(4), 293–310.

Hegel, G. W. F. (2003, reprint). *The phenomenology of the mind.* Mineola, NY: Dover Publications.

King, T. (2003). *The truth about stories: A native narrative.* Toronto: House of Anansi Press Inc.

Kivunja, C. (2014). Theoretical perspectives of how digital natives learn. *International journal of higher education, 3*(1), 94–109.

Palmer, P. (2016). CBC interview with Mary Hines—Tapestry. Retrieved May 2, 2016 from http://www.cbc.ca/radio/tapestry/against-intolerance-1.3494557.

Patterson, J., Goens, G., and Reed, D. (2009). *Resilient leadership for turbulent times: A guide to thriving in the face of adversity.* Lanham, MD: Rowman & Littlefield.

Robertson, H. (2005). Lost in translation. *Phi Delta Kappan,* 410–411.

Rose, E. (2010). Continuous partial attention: Reconsidering the role of online learning in the age of interruption. *Educational technology, 50*(4), 41–46.

Shields, C. M. (2018). *Transformative leadership in education: Equitable changes in an uncertain and complex world.* New York: Routledge.

Shakespeare, W. in Evans, G. B. (1974). *The Riverside Shakespeare.* Boston: Houghton Mifflin.

Wente, M. (2018). The migration crisis will shatter Europe. *The Globe and Mail.* Retrieved from https://www.theglobeandmail.com/opinion/article-the-migration-crisis-will-shatter-europe/.

Wood, G. (2020, December online issue). The next decade could be worse: A historian believes he has discovered iron laws to predict the rise and fall of societies. He has bad news. *The Atlantic,* https://apple.news/AKxVO_7gETX6H0L653_Gq2w.

Chapter 2

The Blurry Path of Leadership in 2020

The year 2020 began as most years do. Global celebrations were broadcast live through multiple mediums. Fireworks scorched the skies in Asia, Europe, and eventually lit up the East Coast of the United States and Canada. The annual release of the Times Square New Year's glitter ball in the heart of New York City was as spectacular as ever, and the people on the screen appeared to be enjoying the Big Apple festivities. There was hope and optimism in the air (https://www.youtube.com/watch?v=mSwM4r22Qs). Even watching the festivities on television was inspiring.

But what can a screen really communicate? The rhythm of life in 2020 was set to start up within a politically and socially divided landscape that seemed oddly and unmistakably unpredictable. Considering the events of the past century, the year 2020 would become a year like no other sending the world into a turbulent tailspin.

THE TRAJECTORY OF A TURBULENT YEAR

In Canada, over five million children would soon be back in front of their teachers (https://www.statcan.gc.ca/eng/dai/smr08/2018/smr08_220_2018 #a1) to resume their learning, extracurricular activities, and social networking. Yet. something was amiss in this dark, cold northern country at the start of January. On the ground, Indigenous protests were taking shape that would put a halt on railway commercial transportation and effectively impact the Canadian economy. Black Lives Matter protests continued across North America and would heat up with the killing of George Floyd in May. As terrible and tragic as these societal issues are and remain, the global event that brought the world to its knees and closed schools, paralyzed governments, forced citizens into lockdown, and stalled economies could not even be seen, except in the fear and suffering that unfolded.

The first mention of COVID-19 arrived in North America through a grainy video on news cycles from a doctor within the city of Wuhan, China. The exact timelines were distorted due to the constant barrage and repetition of messaging from media sources racing to find truth. Perhaps the approximate truth is that the video message was produced and disseminated by the doctor sometime in December 2019 through his social media accounts, and recent accounts peg the virus to have started in November 2019. As the world slowly woke to the distant, but imminent threat, the Chinese doctor came under scrutiny by his government, was later exonerated, and then sadly died from being infected by the disease he was trying to save his patients from, and warn the global community about.

Still, everyone experiences threats differently and that was the case in Canada and the United States where politicians and their civil service initially downplayed the possibility of infection in North America (Gangel, Herb, & Stuart, 2020, September 9; https://www.ctvnews.ca/health/coronavirus/trump-knew-coronavirus-was-deadly-but-wanted-to-play-it-down-bob-woodward-book-1.5097965). And thus, life went on for North Americans in January and February. Planes departed and landed, cruise ships sailed, businesses operated as usual, and students continued to attend schools, colleges, and universities. Then the rhetoric began to change as the virus crept closer to North American soil. Grocery stores got busier. Then they got even busier. Stock items like toilet paper, disinfectant wipes, flour, and sugar became scarce and then all at once, unavailable. Conflicts happened in line-ups and the six-foot social distancing policy came into effect. There is no need to reference any of this, because in some way, shape, or form, it occurred, and everyone experienced it everywhere on the planet.

In March 2020, winter cruise ships saw increasing numbers of virus infections and many opulently decorated vessels could not find port to release their terrified passengers onto land. Airline traffic was rerouted between countries due to high case numbers. And then in Canada, the prime minister's wife became infected and the country appeared to take the disease more seriously and prepare for the turbulence and uncertainty it would bring full scale in the unfolding months.

All businesses that did not fall into the category as essential shuttered their doors and laid off their employees. The arduous process of applying for government assistance began. Schools, colleges, and universities closed. Educators at all levels finished their terms through distance online teaching and learning pedagogies.

THE EXAMINATION OF A PANDEMIC

In late 2020, there are many writers—academic, professional, and amateur—capturing their own observations and building multiple theories about the virus and its fallout and impact on society. Everyone's story is slightly different depending how they observed their world and chose to understand it. The textual layers of COVID-19 do not seem to stop as humanity will have to run its full examination on this once-in-a-lifetime event in the decades to come.

So far, it is being compared to the plagues of the past, most notably the Spanish Influenza outbreak after the First World War that left the world ravaged 100 years ago. Indeed, there will be hundreds, if not thousands of articles, books, documentaries, podcasts, and other emerging mediums focused squarely on interrogating and understanding the COVID-19 virus. It will occupy this generation's collective social mindset. When the writing for this book began, COVID-19 turbulence had not been factored into the analysis of rapid change by educators, school leaders, and students. It is not an event that can be passed up or by, but it still cannot occupy the sole focus of this book. It is just one more hurdle.

First and foremost, this book is about leadership and how individuals in the world of public-school education respond to rapid change. Certainly, COVID-19 has handcuffed leaders, teachers, and students along with their families who rely on a robust and equitable education system everywhere. In 2020, the virus is just one more complexity that school stakeholders have faced among many, and it will be overcome. A vaccine will be discovered. In fact, by the time this book is published, there will be several vaccines being administered to people around the globe.

A second wave of the virus will threaten every business and institution as the first wave did. In fact, it did, and governments and public institutions worked to hold their ground against the invisible disease. The most important thing is to discover how people in schools have responded to this current challenge and other ones. In fact, at the rewriting stage of this very paragraph, the virus is full on into its second stage and schools are now starting to shut down again sending educators and students into the online learning world.

Sadly, there is chaos everywhere. It is November 26, 2020. But all the world's a stage and the show must go on, suggested Shakespeare long ago. It is just important to address what is happening moment by moment near the end of 2020. That is this writer's world. Perhaps it is yours.

So COVID-19 will simply factor into this book as one more challenge that students, parents, principals, vice principals, teachers, teaching assistants, school counselors, bus drivers, custodians, and school volunteers must confront, struggle through, and overcome. It is significant and cannot be understated. Make no mistake, reader. The virus and its aftermath have left a huge wake (think of a speedboat on a lake going sixty miles per hour and the water behind it) in its path. For space enthusiasts, the speed and impact of the virus may be akin to a meteorite hitting a planet. It will be overcome.

School personnel will get stronger; students will keep learning and reach their goals. Life will go on and though there are hundreds of thousands of causalities to this day, humans prevail. Humans are resilient. But it is important to leave this part of the story for now and talk about leadership. Leadership by administrators. Leadership from teachers. And perhaps most important, leadership performed by students who are, without question, the leaders of the future.

THE BLURRINESS OF LEADERSHIP

Another book about leadership? It is a question or statement near the front of many books about leadership. On a shelf nearby, there are over 100 books directly titled about leadership, administration, leaders, and administrators. There are another 100 or so that tap into leadership constructs indirectly in some way. Why is there such an interest in leadership? How does leadership differ from administration?

The answers vary depending on how people learn to look at or choose to look at and understand and ultimately respond to the social realities in their lives. Some people argue that leadership is narrow and that anyone can lead. But in 2020, humans learned that leadership is not narrow, and it is very much required. Some argue that everyone can serve in leadership roles. They can and they cannot. And if you are an individual who spends any amount of time in a school, it becomes obvious that it takes a different kind of human being to lead one or be a leader.

Schools are complex organizations. Not everyone can lead; not everyone can teach. And yet, leaders in schools are surrounded by leaders of various types and from various levels of their school organization. They must be, or the school cannot function effectively for very long.

It was Chris Hodgkinson (1991) who wrote that, "every member of the organization both has and ought to have some element of leadership responsibility" (p. 158). His is a bold claim, but it has stood the test of time since he wrote that line and it is an idea that must be embraced at this period of human history. Otherwise, we are in deep trouble with our institutions, especially in schools. One human cannot organize and lead a school alone. Not in 2020 and certainly not afterward. Not even if it is a smaller rural school far from a large center.

But for the moment, the reader is encouraged to suspend that idea and imagine a person who could lead a school by themselves. What would that person look like? What would that person value? What would motivate them? How might they understand purpose and moral commitment as part of their service? How might that individual communicate to the members within that learning community and wider societal spheres? Still perhaps, the more interesting question is how would the members respond to the communication and to the leadership being expressed?

Most humans enjoy having a say in the way things are run and it is no different in a school. If a leader will not listen to the ideas that are constantly being transmitted across all boundaries, both visible and invisible, then there will most definitely be a breakdown in communication; the school culture will become contaminated to some degree, and any amount of contamination could affect the learning environment which could be costly to the students in the long run. There are so many fashionable leadership approaches, perspectives, and descriptions (Davies, 2009). They all make sense and illuminate human interaction and leadership to some degree in various contexts.

For this book, shared and inclusive leadership will be bound together as a collective leadership possibility and will be the go-to terminology for the extent of this discussion in this book in this part of our history—2020. Not that it is better than say invitational leadership (Novak, 2009), constructivist leadership (Lambert, 2009), ethical leadership (Starratt, 2009), or even entrepreneurial leadership (Hentschke, 2009). Those are all very interesting and important leadership approaches that generously factor into collective leadership strategies.

After all, people can become empowered with additional challenge and responsibility in their lives as they observe how their actions can positively impact lives. And that must be a collective effort; it cannot rest on one person's shoulders to distribute the responsibility and the accolades that go with leading and being led. The very notion of distributing leadership among members of a school implicitly suggests that direct power is the utility of the leader or leaders, knowingly and possibly worse, unknowingly.

REDUCE THE POWER IN THE RELATIONSHIP

At this juncture, it is important to run interference with power and disrupt its reach and grasp as it exists between formal leaders and informal leaders in schools. What must emerge is the idea of empowerment. Leaders, especially principals and vice principals, have power and how they choose to use it will determine the effectiveness of their leadership and the collective efficacy and mindset of their followership. Power and leadership are strange and necessary bedfellows and history teaches humans (if they indulge in history learning) that they can never be separated.

Power is a topic that has been given much time and space and learners of leadership must examine it from all angles and viewpoints. Still, it is not a core theme of this book. It is important indeed, but any interested reader can examine multiple theories related to the evolution, utilization, and consequences of power. Therefore, it will be cast off for now and revisited at different points in this book if it is relevant to that section. This book cannot be about power wielders who burn through resources and people as Burns (1978) has brilliantly illuminated; the thesis here is about empowerment wielders, especially in times of rapid change. To the point.

There are many definitions of leadership that draw upon a person's values, motives, and purpose. But collective leadership in this book requires a definition that strongly considers empowerment, purpose, and motives that serve the collective interest of a social group (such as those who call a school home each day) and builds community, not divides it, or creates any amount or substance of divisiveness. For that reason, the ideas here will draw considerably on Burns's (1978) definition of leadership:

> Leaders inducing followers to act for certain goals that represent the values and the motivations—the wants and needs, the aspirations and expectations—of both leaders and followers. And the genius of leadership lies in the manner in which leaders see and act on their own and their followers' values and motivations. (p. 19)

People may not be aware of leaders or even understand that leadership is operating in any given situation, and that is the reason leadership is blurry. However, people always notice when leadership is absent as when the "shit hits the fan," so to speak. In the past twenty years, which will serve as a flexible timeline for this part of the book's argument, the shit has hit the fan often and from all directions for educators and leaders. The year 2020 is a testament to this fact. One needs to look no further than the surge in social media and digital technologies the past twenty years in our society as one prime example of complexity to which educators and leaders continually respond to and navigate through each school day.

It might be any number of the social media streams where students digitally exist and communicate with their peers—either positively or negatively. It might be a parent wondering when a classroom or the school web page will be updated so they can find out what their child must do for homework or what is going on at the school. One must wonder in 2020 whether the phenomenon is social media magnificence or just another level of societal madness? More on that one later, but for the moment, it is both and the argument that will be laid out will show the reader several social realities of 2020 that educators and leaders are navigating through. But first, it is important to illustrate two earlier ideas made in this chapter.

EMPOWERMENT WIELDERS AS COLLECTIVE LEADERS: THE CASE OF THOM GORDON

Thom Gordon (a pseudonym) is a blurry leader. He had done just about everything in his life by the time he became a lead school custodian. He had worked for the county, operated his own businesses, farmed the land, and performed and served in many other jobs. Now he drove a school bus and managed the hygienic protocol in the building, in addition to ensuring the school water and heating appliances functioned efficiently and safely. That was his job description but only part of his job. His job, one might say, was blurry.

Each morning when students arrived, Thom was at the front door greeting each one that entered. It was the same after school. Gordo, as the students respectfully called him, waited until he had greeted the last student out the door before he boarded his full bus to take his students home safely on his route.

In education, there are often clear and written distinctions between a school's professional staff and their support staff, and often it creates divisiveness between adults. Even children get in on the game when one of the support staff attempts to manage their behavior. Many students view and understand the social hierarchies in society—barriers that contribute to disrespect. Using these lenses, students often respond to support staff who attempt to help them regulate their behaviors with, "you're only the janitor" or "you're a teaching assistant, I don't have to listen to you."

Gordo was not guided by these socially constructed rules; he provided leadership that the students, and all the adults in the school, needed and relied on. When the adults needed someone to talk to and that could be trusted, they turned to Gordo. When students got into trouble, and it could be serious trouble associated to smoking, skipping classes, or conflict with their educators (teachers and assistants), they would seek out Gordo to support them. And he supported the students, unconditionally.

Gordo did not try to restrict or soften the consequences that students needed to face and work through from their infractions. But he did make sure that the teacher or the administrator did not overreact in the situation, especially when the tension and conflict seemed insurmountable in the given situation.

"C'mon Mr. Harnish, you were a student once and you weren't perfect. You need to release your personal feelings in this moment and focus on this student and realize that this is an educational moment in their lives," Gordo would argue. He would be right. This was a blurry moment and leadership was being employed by Gordo with kindness, compassion, and empathy. He was not overstepping his boundaries; he was taking adult-like responsibility in the school where he was working, for the student(s) that he too . . . he too . . . was serving.

Gordo helped coach a sports team each year and drove the bus for many other teams and athletes in the school. He plowed snow in the winter, helped build school greenhouses, and traveled on trips as a school chaperone when enough adults couldn't be found, especially to the dangerous places where campfires and grizzly bears were part of the proactive measures and safety guidelines for the educational trip.

Gordo had his own mentor group with students in it representing Grades 1–12. He attended staff meetings and the adults would often turn to him for his wisdom. He knew the community cold. In brief, Gordo was a leader. No one asked him to be a leader; his job description did not say leader; his pay did not reflect the extended services he provided the school and his community. He never complained about it.

Gordo had enormous influence and power within the learning community, and he protected everyone that he could through the ways he could empower. He released that power and influence by building people up wherever and whenever he could. He was an empowerment-wielder. He never read Hodgkinson, but Gordo was clearly providing leadership in the school from the standpoint of his custodian/bus driver/coach/chaperone/student and teacher advocacy roles. It was all blurry, but significant to the success of the school programs.

Gordo was not only part of the school educational and leadership collective; he played an instrumental role in fashioning the authentic and collective leadership that was present in the school. His leadership transcended the school boundary, deep into the large rural community catchment area the school served. During his time in his various roles at the school, pretention, so often accompanying educators who overtly or secretly harbor inflated ideas about their teaching and identities, did not exist.

Where administrators often lack the courage to address such pretention that might ignite a small rebellion from teachers and assistants, Gordo would sniff it out and humbly serve as a leveling factor. Gordo did not read or discuss the latest theories of education and leadership, but he enacted them through his omniscient and gentle presence in the building. Then came the biggest challenge the school ever faced. He retired.

What Gordo had helped create during his service could not be sustained. Another leader came in, and then another, and then another. Key school personnel retired or migrated to other schools. Sadly, the collective leadership dissipated. But it had existed, and it worked. And that is the point in this story. The possibility of leadership from every corner, every nook and cranny in the building and even outside of it throughout the community, is always present and waiting to be released like horses looking over the gate at the fields beyond.

Leadership is blurry, but a principal, vice principal, educator, and teaching assistant—bluntly, the adults in the building—must be constantly on the lookout and in recruitment mode to allow blurry collective leadership, yet possibly unimagined by them, but no less there, to take root, germinate, and live within the lifeworld of the learning community (Sergiovanni, 2000).

Every school has a Gordo in some form. What this means is a paid or unpaid individual not officially assigned to the standard leadership role of administrator, teacher, or sports coach. Take a minute and think about that unsung and unheralded individual or group of people in your school that have not been invited or encouraged to lead. Unlike Gordo, that is what those individuals might require—encouragement and prodding to lead. They contribute to the team and the evolution of the collective. So much more can be achieved beyond one formal leader. Leaders and educators must break down the blurriness.

OKAY, COLLECTIVE LEADERSHIP . . . SO WHAT?

This section needs to begin with a question, rather than a statement. Why must schools be collective leadership social environments in 2020 and beyond? Reader, this is your cue and encouragement to think beyond the obvious points? Some obvious points include: an administration team cannot be everywhere all at once. That is correct. Administration teams are now, more than ever, out of their buildings at district meetings or in the community advocating for their schools. That is true. Who is leading the school then?

Leadership development must take place at every level in the school for leadership sustainability to have any chance. Just think about Gordo's retirement and what happened afterward. Further, authoritative or a constant directive leadership approach breaks the spirit, motivation, and purpose of the key actors in the school. A bold claim perhaps, but it does. It REALLY does.

The only people who argue against that claim are authoritarian-type leaders and their immediate subordinates who think they are getting things completed single-handedly or in tandem (VPs cannot be exonerated here), when in fact they are actually eroding the school culture and interfering with student learning while they are in the process of creating unpleasant conditions for compliance-only teachers and teacher assistants. That is what authoritarian school leadership delivers. It crushes the teaching and learning spirit in everyone.

Now, a solid comparative might be borrowed from amateur and even professional sports. A coach that constantly yells and berates her or his players eventually gets tuned out to the point that no one is listening to the coach anymore. The players go through the motions. They play out the season. It is not memorable. And that is what happens to teachers and students in an unhappy working environment. Authoritative leadership is not sustainable, and it will not last. One only must investigate history for abundant lessons about this certainty.

To reiterate, that is what happens in a school with a singularly focused leader or administration team. Communication is most often one way, compliance is expected and often shrouded in best interests of the school and students (and it is often only to promote the authoritarian leader's agenda), and discussion of topics at staff or professional learning (PL) meetings is nonexistent or even worse, brief.

It is brief because people think they are being heard. It suggests to people that they were heard only for them to see their ideas dismissed and disregarded. Because if people get to speak up about something, they start to believe that the leaders are finally listening to them. They become frustrated and feel let down when their ideas are not taken seriously or as substantive. They leave meetings wondering, "Why have meetings at all?"

Education for the students then becomes thin in a growing toxic environment like this because people notice this type of leadership style and people talk. They talk here and there throughout the building—first secretly, then openly. They talk beside their cars in the parking lot before they go home, in aisles in their grocery store, and today—worst of all—school personnel are taking their grievances up on social media (which we will get to shortly). Authoritative-type leaders do not like this type of talk or social behavior, and to be fair, it is justifiably unprofessional conduct.

That is what happens when the authoritarian leader runs everything of significance to the school through themselves, when the leader allows it to happen, and it happens most definitely when they do not allow people to engage in dialogue about what is going on or about to occur in their school that they care about. Lord, a book can be filled with anecdotes on authoritative leadership styles. But to the point.

Empowering people to lead in the school collective, to become better, to have purpose in what they are doing, or more importantly, to help them regain their purpose for teaching and service when they lose it. Educators learn early that if they stay in education for a long time, they will most definitely be challenged to hold on to their purpose due to all the evolving complexities of our society. Should these not be priorities of the principal and their administration team?

The only way forward is leading together. Collectively. To empower and challenge the student who hates attending school to become a leader in a way that they can. To tell them they have a purpose. To show them that they need a purpose if you must. They are breathing and living souls, and the world needs them in some way. They just must find it and the collective leader can help them do that.

Going forward in education post 2020, leadership must be collective. And that leadership will draw from inclusive leadership, democratic leadership, invitational leadership, shared leadership among many more. Just look for them. Not one of these approaches will work by itself. A leader needs leaders around them, and they need to arm themselves with all the leadership tools they can. To actively search and find the leadership that exists within the learning community and even in the wider community. A leader needs to look everywhere for leadership in 2020. Here's another story of blurry, unexpected collective leadership. Everyone loves an unexpected gift at an unexpected time.

THE CASE OF MOHAMMED

Mohammed was walking his son to his classroom when he acknowledged the administrator in the hallway. They had attended a community meeting together previously and recognized each other. The administrator was busy hurrying the straggler students into their classrooms on this first day of the year and greeting teachers good morning.

When he returned to his office after circulating the school, Mohammed was waiting for him with a smile on his face. They shook hands, recalled how they had seen each other at the meeting, and the administrator was sorry they did not make introductions then. Mohammed acknowledged the gesture and then asked, "can I speak with you?"

"For sure. How can I help you?" The administrator replied, wondering if his son had a problem on the way to school.

"Mr. Hill, you cannot help me. I am fine. But I think I can help you."

The administrator was slightly bewildered with the invitation and replied, "Oh, how can you help me?"

For the next few minutes, Mohammed explained that he was free during the day, and if the school required help with the new Canadian children and their parents, he had time.

"I work at the plant at night from 11:00 p.m. until 7:00 a.m. You can call me anytime during the day. If I am sleeping, my wife will wake me and I will come over," he said.

The administrator was curious about the nature of help Mohammed could offer. "Okay, that is very kind of you and for sure, we often need parent volunteers to help out on school trips, during our hot lunches, and in the spring track and field. I will definitely call on you." Mohammed's smile got bigger and bigger and he started to giggle.

"No, Mr. Hill. That is not what I meant, but I can help in some of that stuff also. I speak nine languages. If you need help communicating with students or their parents, you can call me, and I will be right over."

There was a pause in the conversation. It was apparent that the administrator had a hard time grasping what Mohammed had said. Nine languages! How was that possible? Perhaps the administrator did not believe Mohammed, for he awkwardly replied, "Ahhh, that is very kind of you, but I think we will be fine and if I need your help, I will be sure to contact you."

There was the smell of arrogance in the administrator's response and it contaminated the air. There was awkwardness and something that tasted like distrust. Why did bias and prejudice emerge through a generous invitation? Was it racial? Was it cultural? Mohammed's giggle came back to a smile and his eyes averted downward. He then looked back into the administrator's eyes. They talked around the invitation, shook hands, and parted from each other.

Mohammed offered an important gift, unselfishly, but the administrator's initial response was to turn away when he should have turned immediately into him and accept the invitation. In short time, racial, linguistic, and cultural conflict occurred rapidly in the diverse school community and he stumbled through them until he dispensed with his pride, arrogance, and stupidity and made the call to Mohammed to accept his invitation. And as he had suggested and voluntarily stated, Mohammed supported the school community in multiple complex situations.

THE LEADERSHIP IS OUT THERE
IN ALL THE COMMUNITIES

Once again, leadership emerged in a blurry moment. Or was it that the administrator made what was clearly apparent, a kind and generous offer of important leadership for the diverse school, blurry? This is but one example of how school leaders let the power in the position guide their thinking and responses, when it fact they should welcome all the leadership from the communities to grow the collective strength, particularly from the newer and long-standing immigrant and minority communities that are sadly overlooked and taken for granted by the dominant Eurocentric world.

Instead of fixating on power and doubt in the moment, the leader should have inquired more about the difficulty in learning nine languages and what an amazing skill set that provides a human being in the contemporary world. That line of conversation develops the dialogue, allows trust to take root, and keeps both adults sealed in a relationship without power. Or, at least, it starts to reduce the power that the administrator holds over the learning community.

This part certainly needs more examination, but it is important to move on. So, the lesson becomes, if you are part of a leadership team whose school community comprises multiple cultures, languages, religions, and worldviews, take the leadership support when it is kindly offered. If it is not offered, then you must enter all the communities, strive, and seek to find it, and do not yield until you have it. Thank you, Tennyson. Otherwise, you will encounter a world of complexity and turbulence that you will not understand fully, if ever, and you will not be able to bring your students and extended community together authentically.

So, as Gordo illustrated to us how to be an untraditional, unheralded, and authentic collective leader inside the school, Mohammed has provided similar imagery from outside the school. Both are key players in the success of a school in 2020. Find your own Gordo and Mohammed. There is more evidence for collective leadership in 2020 and it confronted North American society on September 29, 2020. But in a real-time, different way.

THE GREAT DEBATE—CAN A LOUD COMMUNICATOR REALLY LEAD?

Gordo must wonder how students are trying to understand what they witnessed on live television, or on their computers, or even streamed through their smartphones (patience, patience reader, we will get to technology shortly) during the first United States presidential debate September 29, 2020 that led to the United States 2020 election. Yes, Canadians watched the debate also, as what happens in the United States impacts every Canadian directly in some way.

At that moment, each candidate challenged to lead what is arguably the most powerful country in the world. Leadership at its height in our current world might just be embodied in the historical institution of the American president. This is certainly the case in the Western Hemisphere.

Consider everything that has been written in books, articles, news stories and such, and add on many motion pictures that have been based directly or indirectly on the American president as an ethical, heroic, collective, and quite personable leader (*Air Force One* and *Independence Day* come to mind), and it might illuminate how the North American public on all sides of political persuasions and ideologies view their top national leader.

It is the same in Canada, but we do not have the movies to back it up. People expect their president and prime minister to be better than them. They at least expect them to be better, period. At the very least, it is not a bold claim to suggest citizens on both sides of the 49th parallel expect their leaders to not be embarrassing.

Now, it is not an immediate intention to chastise either political candidate on that moment in late September, and in this chapter, neither of them will be named because they are known. Should this book get published in 2021, one of them will be in power and one of them will slip into a slow oblivion, their legacy lost from the mindset of the country, the only trace of memory from this moment in time.

The spectacle was funny at times, but mostly terrifying when the speculative imagination went forward into the next presidential term. Can leaders bully at the national international level? Should national leaders yell and scream at each other, interrupt the flow of dialogue, and make personal attacks on family members? Has leadership really come to this in 2020? Everyone and every group seem to have their own interpretation of the event in isolation. But what does it really mean?

It means that loud bullies eventually lose. In fact, they lose everything. They learn that they do not matter as much as the people they are chosen by to lead them. They become impotent. Yelling and screaming and beating one's chest to suggest dominance, to promote fear and mistrust, is to mislead. Down the rabbit hole they must fall. Choose collective, authentic, ethical, inclusive leadership. The world needs people to work together to lead post-2020.

CHAPTER 2 ACTIVITIES AND QUESTIONS

1. How did you and your professional colleagues respond to COVID-19? What are some of the valuable lessons you were able to take forward in your service?
2. Can one person be the sole leader in a school? Have a debate.
3. How would you define collective leadership? Is there a better leadership approach in 2020? If so, what?
4. How might collective leadership intersect with invitational, entrepreneurial, constructivist, and transformative leadership approaches?

5. Who are the unsung collective leadership agents in your school or workplace? What do they do that makes them stand out in your mind?

REFERENCES

Burns, J. M. (1978). *Leadership.* New York, NY: Harper and Row.

Davies, B. (2009). Introduction: The essentials of school leadership. In B. Davies (Ed.), *The essentials of school leadership* (pp. 1–12). Thousand Oaks: Sage.

Gangel, J., Herb, J., & Stuart, E. (2020, September 9). Trump knew coronavirus was "deadly" but wanted to "play it down": Bob Woodward book. *CNN story on CTV Online news.* Retrieved September 9, 2020 from https://www.ctvnews.ca/health/coronavirus/trump-knew-coronavirus-was-deadly-but-wanted-to-play-it-down-bob-woodward-book-1.5097965

Hentschke, G. (2009). Entrepreneurial leadership. In B. Davies (Ed.), *The essentials of school leadership* (pp. 147–165). Thousand Oaks, CA: Sage.

Hodgkinson, C. (1991). *Educational leadership: The moral art.* Albany, NY: SUNY Press.

Lambert, L. (2009). Constructivist leadership. In B. Davies (Ed.), *The essentials of school leadership* (pp. 112–132). Thousand Oaks, CA: Sage.

Novak, J. (2009). Invitational leadership. In B. Davies (Ed.), *The essentials of school leadership* (pp. 53–73). Thousand Oaks, CA: Sage.

Sergiovanni, T. J. (2000). *The lifeworld of leadership: Creating culture, community, and personal meaning in our schools.* San Francisco, CA: Jossey-Bass.

Starratt, R. (2009). Ethical leadership. In B. Davies (Ed.), *The essentials of school leadership* (pp. 74–90). Thousand Oaks, CA: Sage

Chapter 3

1999–2020: Wrestling with Darkness

The young student always arrived around 7:30 each morning before the bus students started to arrive at 8:20. She would put away her personal and school belongings in her Junior High locker and then walk down the hallway to the main office where she would greet the administrator, who was early to work. "Good morning Mr. Henry. Can I please go and work on a computer in the lab?" It was her morning ritual that occupied her until her friends arrived.

At this time most mornings, several teachers were in their classrooms completing their preparation for the day's teaching and activities, the custodians were applying last minute hygienic detail to their areas in the school, and if there was a sports season like volleyball or basketball going on that month, a team could be heard practicing in the large gymnasium. And, even though the shock waves of the Littleton, Colorado, high school mass shooting the previous April was still being felt across North American schools and communities, this rural Canadian community was safe and secure by all threat assessment measures in October near the end of the twentieth century.

The school was opened and unlocked by 6:00 a.m. when the first custodian arrived, and it usually was not secured until long into the evening after the last practice or community event was over. Sometimes, though not often, the last adult left the school and forgot to lock the front door. Though it caused a bit of a stir, it was generally laughed off by the staff as they were gently reminded to check the door each evening before they left. School lockdowns, threat assessment protocols, and training for both were still a future invention, but not far off. This was 1999 in rural Canada, but an argument could be made that it could be in any agricultural rural area across North America.

The administrator looked forward to the student's greeting each morning while he worked on organizing and transcribing all the attendance slips from the day before into a running record file on his admin work computer. This allowed him to track student attendance over a twenty-four-hour period and call parents if he was concerned about attendance patterns with any of the 600 students. The student was cheerful, well-behaved, and a strong learner and leader in class.

The administrator knew this to be true because he taught her in one of her core courses. Letting her into the computer lab was not a big deal he believed, as the computer teacher had not informed him of any problems that she had caused with her early morning presence. As he unlocked the door and let her into the room, he said, "See you later in class."

1999—Digital Communication Begins for the Leader

At 8:10 he received a phone call from an angry teacher in another of the district's schools located ten miles away. The teacher was upset because one of her students was working on a computer in their school's computer lab that morning and had received a nasty, obscenity-filled, and highly inappropriate message from a student from the administrator's school.

The administrator was stunned and did not know who that student could be but gave the teacher his word that as soon as all the students arrived, he would get to the bottom of it and find out who wrote the message. His immediate assumption was that it was in printed letter form and mailed through the post. The teacher said, "No, the student is in your school right now!" The administrator asked her how that was possible when the letter was probably sent a couple of days ago for her student to have it this morning. He knew that it took at least that amount of time for the mail to reach their school from wherever it was sent, even if it was sent within the same region. It took time.

Again, he assured the teacher, who was now very frustrated with him and his listening skills, that he would follow up. Then she said something that would shake his leadership world.

"The letter came through an email from the student who is working right this very minute in your computer lab. She had a back and forth with our student and our student showed me the email just now. I am sending you a print-off copy of the email to your fax machine." And the teacher hung up the phone.

He waited several minutes by the new fax machine in the main office for its start-up hum and rattle. He thought that the fax machine would knock out the postal service. It never did. Soon, a paper slid from the loading tray into the rollers and slowly made its way through the machine where the wonders of instant communication became both enlightening and frightening for the young administrator. It was 1999. In his hands was concrete evidence of what the teacher had been describing, but he still had trouble comprehending the entire email transmission process.

It was clearly a typed message with several mistakes in it, not really a letter as his mind had constructed one. Several words and phrases were written with extreme and vulgar expression with exclamation marks emphasizing the adolescent wrath of the sender. It was as the teacher in the other school had stated—a highly offensive and targeted message at the receiver. Now he had an unpleasant task and one for which he did not truly prepare for, or even follow his educational leadership instincts into the position and responsibilities that he now held.

As he walked the young student back to his office, both were visibly somber and forlorn. He at having to phone her parents and inform them of their daughter's misconduct and explain that he would set up an in-school suspension that he would monitor over the next two days. He would not send her home for this infraction but instead, look for alternate educative moments over the next two days to work with her. She was forlorn at being caught and breaking the trust she had with the administrator, as she now knew her early morning computer time was jeopardized. Yet, both would learn that all was not lost. It would indeed end up as an educative digital moment. It was 1999.

The student was productive over the two days at her desk in the time-out room, buried at the back of the school in a book room. The administrator collected her work from her teachers and returned it to them when she had completed it. In all fairness, her teachers could not keep her busy and that is what the administrator was hoping for. It always amazed him at how much a junior high student could produce if their distractions were limited and you could harness one of the many energies they possessed.

Near the end of the second day, the administrator walked down to the book room and told the student to pack up her books and binders, place them in her locker, and meet him at his office where they would talk about the event once more. Together, they would go over her apology letter that she wrote while in her in-school suspension before it was sent through district courier so that it would get to the student the following week. An apology over email seemed inflammatory to the open wound she had created given the context of the situation.

The administrator noted that it was evident that the student was sincerely sorry for the mean message and she promised that she would not send any other inappropriate emails in the future. The administrator believed her, and during his time in the school, she never did while she was in that computer lab.

The in-school suspension now over, there was still twenty minutes left before the last class was let out and the buses would be boarded for home. The administrator intentionally planned this last twenty minutes because his superintendent was telling all the district administrators that they needed to improve their digital communication skills this year. This twenty minutes with the student at the end of the week was an intentional leadership act for the young administrator and would change his professional life and course of his career. He gently asked her, "Can you please teach me how to write and send an email?" It was 1999.

THE PRE-DIGITAL DARK AGE

There is much that can be learned from the story. First, it is loosely based on an event that took place in October 1999. In the years around the end of the twentieth century and beginning of the twenty-first century, communication was changing rapidly in schools, as districts were starting to participate with new ways to reach its stakeholders beyond the phone call, written letter, or memo in a sealed envelope or not, sent home with students in their backpacks. Policymakers and school leaders were looking at different ways to spend taxpayer dollars on more technology, because the free market, computer software industries, and the global world was moving in that direction (Wallerstein, 2005).

Twenty-first century teaching, learning, and leadership would soon become the rage and discourse across education regions around the world and it was not a world that was light years away from being totally digitally connected. It was now and it was happening. Just think, that was 1999 and look at where the world is just twenty-two years later. It is unimaginable. But it happened in one generation.

The story also illustrates and illuminates how children and young adults are often first to home plate, as adults are still rounding second base trying to catch up with them, when it comes to computers, digital technologies, and social media. But more on that last one in moment. Young brains are curious and hungry for new things all the time, whether they are good or bad, and when the information superhighway hit North America and the world in the mid- to late 1990s, news makers and modern soothsayers in science boldly told Western consumers how their lives would be changed forever in the next few years. And by golly, they were right!

Clearly, the administrator in the vignette was behind the times and certainly behind the digital capacities the young computer and email savvy student possessed as he required her assistance to learn about constructing and sending digitized transmissions. He was very fortunate that she helped him learn how to write, send, and even receive emails. Again, she displayed leadership in an awkward moment. That is how blurry leadership can be.

"I Found It on the Web"

The late 1990s was also a time when it became common in classroom discussions for students to spin their tales of the websites they were encountering after school, and in their evening online adventures on their personal computer from their desk in the bedroom, or in the kitchen where teen-involved and astute parents could observe the websites their children were visiting. The dark web was already beginning to emerge, and students with internet hookups in their homes had access to all types of websites. Use your imagination here, reader. In the late 1990s, firewalls and filters were still getting tested out by school districts and students could often find themselves visiting inappropriate websites with a click of their mouse in the school computer lab.

Further, the equity issue was still invisible for many educators, but looking back, kids whose parents could afford such technology for their homes were several steps ahead of everyone else. Most students had to wait until their school administration budgeted for the faster optic cable systems to be installed so their school's wiring could be updated so their computer labs could be hardwired directly. In 1999, there were few wireless systems available yet, especially in the far-off rural areas of North America. Look at maps of the Canadian western provinces and western United States. There are a lot of wide-open spaces. And millions of people live and learn there.

Veteran teachers might also remember how much many of their students' work magically improved with the emergence of the internet. There were students who struggled putting two or three sentences together in middle school, who would submit long essays and short stories with amazing punctuation and descriptive vocabulary usage. For the educator who did not understand how this could happen, a phone call to a parent inquiring if they had written the assignment for their child might be the first order of business in pursuit of understanding how their child had improved 50 percent in one unit.

If that inquiry stalled, the student would be asked by the teacher, "Did you really complete this assignment yourself?" "Yes, I did, I found it on the web, and printed it out. I did that all by myself." It was a conundrum that had to be ethically examined and then pedagogically managed. It would all sort out in time when educators learned a lot of what students (and they themselves) had access to on the net.

But getting back to the opening story, email did not magically pop up in 1999; it had been a digital invention years before though the exact year is under constant interrogation. Americans claim that the communication tool was used by its military forces during the end of the Cold War (Graff, 2017). That begs the question—if the United States was using digital technologies for communication through advanced computer technology, were other countries, perhaps North America's Cold War adversary, the Soviet Union, using it also?

One must not get too ethnocentric about who was first to the communication digital dance. The reality is that it existed in some iteration during the Cold War era or at least near the end of the Cold War which can be targeted to the fall of communism and the Soviet Union, as well as its satellite nation allies in the mid- to late 1980s. Still, it did not exist in the way it exists in 2020 of course. The internet was not readily available and the general North American civilian still had to wait a few years to go online and digitally interact with other people.

Cold War Games

But North American citizens got the opportunity to get a snippet of internet possibilities in 1983, when actors Matthew Broderick and Ally Sheedy entertained, amazed, and terrified audiences with their digital mastery in the movie *WarGames* (Badham, 1983). By standard response at the time, their performances set imaginations on fire as the movie gained three Academy Award nominations.

The sophisticated, nerdy, personal computer abilities they possessed allowed them (mostly Broderick's character) to hack into their high school's mainframe computer system and change a bad grade to an A grade. That was the cool part of the story. For every underachieving high school student that year who watched the film (including this author, who graduated from high school in 1983), a vision of changing their own high school grades, locked in as tight as humans in Alcatraz in the school's mainframe computer system, possibly took shape in their minds. It certainly did in this author's case.

The real clincher in the film for this writer was that Broderick's character's computer savvy also enabled him, with the support of Sheedy's character, to prevent a global thermonuclear war. That was the terrifying part of the movie.

Mindful and reflective educators and school leaders who could understand how art often mirrors reality in 1983 must have at least thought about preparing their students for such a world or the type of preparation one might need to live in such a digital and highly interconnected world. If they did not, then they did not pick up on the main theme of the movie related to how computer systems and digital worlds would eventually collide and control human lives, or at least help them better control their own worlds. One can choose their own view on this reality. But in all fairness, it was 1983 and it was all still a few years away. And by 2020, that is the reality.

Yes, the world had been changing socially, economically, environmentally, and culturally since humans began to organize themselves in social groups since time immemorial. And then during the Cold War era prior to the information age, life seemed to speed up as newer technologies made human lives better and more comfortable, at least in the industrialized countries. But everything good often has an evil twin and unfortunately, technology created a much more dangerous world.

To further this last point, the long bow in Europe or on the steppes of Siberia could take out a deer and a human at several hundred feet. Today, a modern battleship protects a shoreline and keeps people safe, but one of its cruise missiles can wipe out an entire city and population. Yin and Yang. Technology is frightening and humans are constantly wrestling with its dark side and viewers came into full contact with that notion through *WarGames* if they had not already by 1983. The Cold War years were very anxiety-inducing for people on the planet.

So, in basic summary, when the industrial revolution took hold of the world, then things really sped up. That idea is not at the core of this book of course, but it brings this argument back to where it was with the student, the administrator, and the email. All of a sudden in or around 1999, the world, which was already going fast, was now going to shift communication gears, but this time, there was no going back . . . at least not for twenty years until the coronavirus stopped everyone on the planet in their tracks. And, that is what this chapter is about. The years 1999–2019. Those twenty years echo a thought 400 years old: "The time is out of joint" (Shakespeare in Evans, 1974).

WRESTLING WITH DARKNESS BEFORE THE CORONAVIRUS: 2000

How did the world get to this point? It would take more than just this book to outline that and the history of communication, industrial, and technological development really is not the scope of this writing. But it all factors in. What is important for educators in 2020 and beyond is to understand how educators and school leaders as well as their students are responding and adapting to the rapid changes, that are part of their lived and living experiences. What do they have to do to thrive beyond 2020?

The story of the inappropriate email is certainly common to the educators nearing the end of their careers in 2020. Emails can still be mischievous, but they have given way to even faster and possibly more potent communication strategies in the adolescent world. Emailing has opened the door to all the social media that currently operate in 2020. Now a person can send a text, tweet, or Facebook post, friendly or otherwise, and have the return message within seconds. A click to post, a beep, bleep, or buzz back. It is instantaneous and that is problematic, especially in schools, which will be addressed later in the chapter.

In 2020, everyone knows this, and it is the speed of the communication that educators and leaders are in most conflict with because they do not have the time to intercept the messages and provide counsel where it is required. High-speed communication only gives them reaction time to make their decisions. It is unfortunate but school leaders are still adjusting to this reality in their schools. They are working hard at catching up to this phenomenon.

Looping back for a moment, computers, and Local Area Networks (LANs), also called computer labs, sprung to life in schools in the 1980s. Yet, by the early 1990s, most schools were still only using computers in small labs and in their administration offices for collecting and inputting basic data like student demographic data, class lists, and attendance records as described in the story. The lucky educator was one who had a computer in their classroom.

Having two or more computers for their students to use was a dream for any educator in the mid- to late 1990s and even a little later. Most educators across North America were not wired for the world until the late 1990s and only the schools whose leaders had a vision for it, and generally in communities and regions that were investing in faster communication technologies. What that meant was regions with robust industries and population bases with good taxation income has better digital service.

There was definitely a lag and in small districts it was not uncommon for parents to take their children out of their home catchment area schools and place them in another school that had more computer hardware and software with savvy teachers who were more advanced and interested in delivering a technology-based education.

These visionaries were everywhere and nowhere all at once. For instance, they could be found in large urban schools surrounded by all the modern amenities a civilization could boast and they could be found out on the distant rural grasslands if that school leader was visionary and foresaw, like Nostradamus perhaps, where the world was heading. The struggle for more and more technology had begun and schools were a primary battlefield in 1999 in an accelerating world (Gleick, 1999). Students became trade bait for schools, and teacher jobs depended on having high numbers of students in their schools and classes. Competition for students became a struggle for schools even within the same districts.

Many teachers in North America understandably would have been ahead of the computer learning curve through their own personal interests in technology. If they were readers, they could capitalize on science journals and magazines that constantly foretold the travel and communication possibilities of future generations.

But most educators, like the administrator in the story, would have still existed in the pre-digital dark age, even though they were familiar with the personal computer and used it for part of their day-to-day work life. The above realities involving communication technology brings to mind a story that was recently told to this author by his uncle when they were discussing the evolution of computer systems and communication. The event occurred at a Canadian university in 1967 and foreshadows how communication technology evolved in the North American context. The story is very interesting and is shared verbatim below:

> Your references to technology in chapter 3 reminded me of a conversation our Computer Science class had with the professor back in 1967. Bear in mind that at that time computers were so large they filled huge rooms and they were not at all consumer-friendly or useful to most people. The professor had emigrated to Canada from Czechoslovakia and was better informed about computers than most people at that time. He told us that the technology existed where a telephone could be connected to a typewriter, television set, and computer. This simple system could be used to see what was on sale at the grocery store, check on available flights and print out airline tickets. These were just a few of his examples. I asked him that if that technology existed, why weren't we using it. His reply astounded me, and I have never forgotten it. He said "It's simple. The world isn't ready for it yet." It makes me wonder what technology has been developed but is gathering dust at the moment because this very well-informed society isn't ready for it yet. (L. Spencer, personal communication, December 11, 2020)

Is the world ready for the next wave of communication technology? That is a very important question in 2020. What is clear is that some leaders were engaged with digital communication technologies earlier than the leader and student in the story that started this chapter, but by early to mid-2000s, email communication was becoming the standard form of communication in schools. Still to this day, email holds the top place in institutional daily communication—though that will be hotly disputed by social media followers.

Even in 2020, school administrators continue to be frustrated when teachers do not check their emails at least once per day, even if they are communicating with additional technologies like text messaging, and social media like Facebook, Twitter, and Instagram. Perhaps it will always be a sore spot with teachers who just want to focus on their students and not worry about the hundreds of emails in their inbox. Leadership will have to figure it out, but it will not be easy as newer communications applications become available.

WRESTLING WITH VIOLENCE IN SCHOOLS

Earlier in this chapter, the Littleton, Colorado, school shooting massacre was briefly referenced and so were the threat assessment protocols that developed after that madness that shook the education world. School shootings have become a constant anxiety for educators and school leaders across North America and, since that tragic day in April 1999, numerous tragedies have occurred. Taber, Alberta, and La Loche, Saskatchewan, in Canada; Newtown, Connecticut, and Parkland, Florida, in the United States are prime examples of where violence has penetrated schools and educator and student mindsets the past twenty years.

It is not a steep climb to argue that the violence impacting schools the past twenty years have kept educators in a state of perpetual anxiety. And it would not be a false claim to suggest that they remain there. Disruption, conflict, and violence is always at the school door waiting to enter. The personifying image is not lovely, but it is true. The internet and social media, if not the major contributing factor to the new social reality associated to school violence, have played at least a leading role right across North America and around the world.

Violence can happen anywhere, anytime. The content uploaded and distributed through the internet and social media communication platforms in various forms can radicalize human minds. It all causes extreme anxiety for educators and their students. This needs some time to unpack. It is a heavy topic.

Social theorists, from the major human social science disciplines, do their best to examine the events and try to explain the elevated levels of violence they are seeing from youth in North America and from around the world. They have not failed in their research mandates. Much of their argument makes sense to the avid reader, viewer, and listener of the ideas they produce. But because human beings are such a complicated social/psychological animal, the theorists are perplexed and search for newer and newer theories to try and explain the human behavior unfolding in the new millennium. They too have not been able to keep up to the societal challenges the past twenty years.

To lay the blame squarely on mass media, consumerism, failed political and social leadership, absent parents, bad educators, access to high powered weapons, and to ultra-violence through video gaming and social media streaming and interaction would be a gross overstatement. Or perhaps an understatement. Take your pick in the paradox. And yet, some, if not all, of these social realities that existed or evolved the past twenty years most surely have contributed to the accelerated level of violence in schools and communities today. And the educators and social theorists know this; it is just difficult for them to explain it. But, it cannot be argued.

School Lockdown Practice

Today, schools not only practice traditional fire drills, they have their students and school personnel (as well as any visitors who might be in the school at the moment of drill) go through school lockdown protocols to practice what to do, where to go, and how to behave if ever there is a potential violent person or worse, an active shooter on location or in the school and community catchment area. Certainly, other writers, both academic and professional, have covered this phenomenon extensively (for instance, engage the multiple websites on the excellent work of Kevin Cameron and his colleagues: https://nactatr.com/team/kevincameron.html), but it is worth a moment here to really give the reader some sense of what effective lockdown practice is like for educators, school leaders, and students.

A school anywhere in the world is an active and exciting social environment. Bodies flow steadily through hallways and classrooms. It is a ripe research context for a critical ethnographer engaged in documenting the minute by minute interactions of humans full of inspiration and perspiration within their environment and what it might ALL mean using thick and rich descriptive language. There are smells, sounds, and gestures that can be seen and felt by anyone.

In each school, there is a heartbeat. For an educator, it is the cultural lifeblood that fills their veins and keeps their respiratory, circulatory, and digestive systems operating with a steady pace and regularity as they go about their teaching and manage their classrooms effectively. It is noisy and even when students are all tucked safely into their rooms with doors shut, the vibrations of teaching and learning can still be heard and felt. It is a collective heartbeat. A lockdown (practice or otherwise) ends it all.

The immediate silence in the school, after everyone freezes, is eerie. One should not be able to hear the buzz of lights and the hum of fans. Students hide under their desks or turn them sideways. This takes effort. People crouch on the toilets in bathrooms and in windowless dark rooms housing the sports and drama equipment. This takes effort. The teacher loses control of students in this moment. They cannot "shush" them; they cannot move a body part; they cannot provide that snake-eye teacher look of disapproval. Any twitch might signal their location. One's ears begin to pulsate. Everyone knows it is practice; still, everyone is terrified that one day they might have to go through the experience in real time. The mind cannot turn off the "what if" scenarios during the drill. It shakes the soul to the core. During the drill, one asks, "How did our society get to this point?"

No social scientist or human behavior theorist can give us that in 2020. At least, not all of it. Maybe they could before, but not now. There is just too much social media noise. Too many internet sites that can spark disillusion and despair. There have been too many shootings around the world. The bullied student. The disengaged student. The vengeful student. The lonely and depressed student. No social researcher will ever be able to fully grasp the fear the school leaders, the educators, and the students feel when they, and perhaps selective colleagues, are the only ones in the school. It is always changing.

And then there are the one or two school leaders quickly roaming the hallways, checking classrooms, the gym, the washrooms, making sure everyone is following protocol, thinking about the what if? What if the perpetrator is around this corner, in that hallway, in the gym right now, or outside trying to get in? Will I be able to take the bullet? How did we get to this point where schools have to practice lockdowns? Why did we get here? Try to answer that and you will only go circular.

The drill is over, the beautiful noise and rhythm of school life and learning returns. But the educators are shaken; some will need a drink after school. The school leader will need a couple. Lessons do not proceed or finish well the day of lockdown practice. Conflict in society, though part of every society, is now in every school, every moment of the day. It stands at the door looking in. It is the possibility of conflict and potential violence. Teachers cannot shield their students from it anymore. Perhaps they still should try to. Perhaps they should not. Yet, conflict is there everyday in the form of student disagreement, parental disagreement with the school or with and between personnel who serve the school and families.

There is teacher to teacher disagreement, and of course the potential of the disenfranchised and angry citizen who had a bad experience in their schooling and serves society as a flashpoint for the news cycles of the day. Why schools? Because even in 2020, schools are still mostly public, mostly still open, and the most vulnerable of our social institutions. They house children. Even with locked doors after everyone arrives in the morning, people still must enter and leave schools.

DIVISIVE COMMUNITIES

S. E. Hinton wrote a wonderful book called *The Outsiders*. If every middle school teacher in language arts has not taught the book in North America, many have surely directed students to it through their additional class reading lists. And, if you are an educator who has not, then you might consider the book for your students in the future. There is also an excellent movie with several high-profile young actors who later made it big in their careers. First though, what is a divisive community and what defines one in 2020?

Division is part of the human experience and has been since the organization of social groups. Again, way too much to cover in this book, but one benchmark example for this writer and reader of history is the human bondage cycle of the past several millennia. Some of the work by Francis Fukuyama (1993) illuminates how humans are trapped by divisiveness related to prestige and the struggle for recognition. It is an excellent read. When you think about that idea, contemporary society and many of its issues really light up. But you will have to read Fukuyama's book yourself and find out how you think about that and what it means to you.

Whether social division is defined by master and slave or indentured worker, or the working underclass of our current era, class divisiveness still extends its tentacles in a myriad of ways in 2020. And S. E. Hinton captured the spirit of class divisiveness remarkably in her story as she and her readers set out on their learning journey to unpack the social divides of a midwestern United States city. Yet, the setting could be anywhere and readers (and viewers of the movie) quickly identify that reality as one of the primary themes the young writer was sharing (Hinton was sixteen years of age when she crafted the book). The rich kids stayed together. The poorer kids stayed together. In the story, crossing the boundaries of either social group was a social taboo and one risked injury or even death if they penetrated the other group's social spaces. Read the book.

In April 1999, social divisiveness cost fifteen people their lives in a school in Colorado. Was the conflict class-based? Was the conflict group-based? It is still best to leave that to the social psychologists and criminologists to place their interpretations on reasons why the event occurred. But the idea for the moment is that human beings are complex animals and the reasons "why" will never be known in absolute terms because there are so many minds and voices trying to understand such events that are taking place all too frequently in or near our nations' school zones. It is a noisy discourse which leaves the school leader walking alone down the hallways each month during the lockdown drill wondering, "what if" and "will I be able to take the bullet?"

The divisiveness that educators and school leaders must navigate through is not only about class and group dynamics within their buildings and classrooms. The divisiveness can be extended to differences in race, culture, language, religion, gender, sexual orientation, or an intersection of two or more. Again, this is not a new phenomenon in our society and there is no such claim being made or put forward in this part of the book. These are the social realities of our rapid times that school administration teams, and the teachers, support staff, students, and parent community members they lead are confronting daily. Everyone associated with a school learning environment is wrestling with some darkness related to one or several intersecting forms of socially divisive human interactions. And there are hundreds, if not thousands of books and research and professional articles produced each year on any of these social realities as they are affecting teaching and learning in schools.

Still, and this is the main point of this part of the chapter, educators and school leaders are ill-prepared to effectively respond to these challenges. That does not mean that the social realities are unknown to them. The argument is one about the type and form of professional learning one must encounter and authentically engage to become professionally prepared and responsive to these school challenges. And currently, education programs are mostly invested with providing the pedagogical know-how to their preservice teachers that will enable them to get a job and begin their teaching career. The rest is up to them and their school districts.

Tomorrow is November 3, 2020

That is right, tomorrow is a big day in North America. Not just for the United States. Canada, Mexico, and even France, with its two small islands off the coast of Newfoundland, are very interested in the outcome of the election between U.S. presidential incumbent Donald Trump and his Democratic opponent, Joe Biden. The months leading up to this moment in human history have been filled with tumultuous events crisscrossing socioeconomic borders that intersect with racially, culturally, and religiously divided communities. The coronavirus is ravaging through many parts of the world, large social justice movements are taking place across North America, and citizens appear to be arming themselves with even more weapons as they await the results.

At the time of writing this paragraph, the tension on November 2, 2020 in North America was suffocating. There was a wait and see game going on. Educators and school leaders are about to confront events that are very difficult to predict. Many stores in the United States have run out of guns and ammunition, and some large department stores have taken guns and ammunition off its shelves in areas of the country that are deemed hot spots only to reverse their decision afterward (Miranda, 2020). Will darkness and a long winter hold 500,000,000 people captive between the Arctic Ocean and the Gulf of Mexico? That will be the start of the next chapter in this book.

Time moves fast. Or, maybe, it is just that things expand so fast that time seems to be moving rapidly catching people unprepared or feeling like they are falling behind. Maybe it has been that way the past 200 years. 400 years. 1,000 years. But it is difficult to agree with that when so much has happened the past twenty years placing humans on the precipice of the unimaginable.

Twenty years ago, the current president of the United States had his own reality television show, and his main moniker was telling participants on the show that "You're fired!" Just over twenty years ago, the Canadian prime minister was a high school drama teacher and he once dressed in a Halloween costume that consisted of painting his face black (Bryden, 2020). The coronavirus has challenged both leaders as well as their political colleagues and supporting bureaucrats since the disease began afflicting their citizens. It is much the same around the world.

But all this begs the question, what kind of leader or leaders do humans require now in 2020? In 2021? Certainly, we need people in leadership positions who will not be divisive in any way. It is too much for the mind to process on this particular day, on the eve of an event that might just ignite flash points of turbulence and violence in both countries. For now, it may be more prudent to return to the young emailer and her administrator and dredge out a lesson or two from the last twenty years.

DARKNESS AND TURBULENCE
CANNOT BE PARALYZING

In 2020, with all the paralyzing and debilitating events occurring in the world, the subheading above might just be the best (or worst) paradox ever constructed. How can leaders, educators, and their students not be in some way shaped, shifted, and sometimes stopped dead in their tracks in 2020 amid any of the realities that dominate the world and have been briefly touched upon in this chapter. Elections, viral outbreaks, civic and economic shutdowns, social unrest and resistance movements, and environmental issues, (to be taken up in chapter four) are just a few of the realities that students, their teachers, and leaders greet each morning when they learn together. It is all inescapable.

A person in leadership has many perspectives from which they can draw additional insight to help them understand the realities and perhaps how best they might respond to them as the previous chapter highlighted. Articles, books, professional journals, webinars, blog posts, social media sites all serve a valuable purpose in leadership development. However, in the runaway society that humans find themselves in today, reading and engaging with web tools might not be part of the timeline for busy leaders and educators, due to time constraints and managing their learning agendas. It is a solid argument and sad at the same time because, educators need to keep reading about leadership, just as writers need to keep writing about it. The social context is forever evolving. Just as it was in 1999 for the young administrator who had never sent an email.

But he asked for help, and help and leadership were there in the form of a young person who happened to be more gifted than he was in creating, sending, and receiving emails. And even though she was caught in a misadventure, and the situation of learning was not optimal in that it arose in a difficult situation, it all worked out. Support was there for the young student through the patience and empathy of her administrator, and help was there for the young administrator through the kindness and inclusive actions of the young student.

Both could have turned away from each other, which unfortunately is all too often the case in such matters of discipline. Instead, both turned toward and into each other to work through the situation. It just cannot be any other way in 2020 and beyond.

Brené Brown (2017) writes, "People are hard to hate close up: Move in" (p. 63). In this author's mind, there is no better suggestion to counter the paralyzing effects of our divisive society in 2020 than the meaning behind those words. It appears people have lost their way with people that do not subscribe to their ideas, to their view of the world, to the norms of the group to which they belong. Whether it is class related or due to race, language, culture, religion, or differences of opinion on what matters about gender identification, people have lost their ways on how to communicate with people.

Conversation has become louder and even more confusing through the digital platforms of the internet. Truths, part-truths, no truth. It could even be framed as lies, part-lies, and all lies, depending on how one chooses to use and employ their perceptions. Conclusively, the strange and complex matter of the social world is at hand. Society is now deep into the marrow of turbulence. Wrestling with darkness in 2020 is the same as it was in 1999. Only it is much faster. And for this writer, it seemed to begin around 2005.

The Digital Nightmare Begins

Imagine you are an educator in the school year 2004–2005. It is approximately when cell phones started to morph into smarter phones. It is also when the first digital social connection platforms showed up and started to entice more and more users. For the curious student who was fortunate enough to have a computer at home hooked up to the internet, the world just got a little more interesting.

For most educators, it got increasingly complex, confusing, and distorted. Further imagine that you are off from teaching in the 2005–2006 school year. You might be enjoying a maternity leave; you might be on an educational or deferred salary leave, or you might be recovering from an illness and just need the time away to get better.

The school year 2005–2006 may be an arbitrary estimation to the reader, but for this educator, in and around this time, more and more students received cell phones and school leaders and classroom teachers were anything but ready to respond to this new phenomenon in their work lives. Now the students could phone their friends in other classes from their desk. Better yet, they could text them and ask them where they would like to hang out at lunch, at the break, or what they were doing after school.

Cell phones beeped, blipped, and jiggled throughout classrooms and educators who were thinking about this started to go nuts. But when change such as this happens gradually, then suddenly, then any type of action is reaction, and usually not in the form of best or better responses. This is especially true when district and school leaders do not see the conundrum as all that complicated when they themselves are using cell phones to call, text, and set up their meetings.

But the situation becomes a crisis when you add in a social media platform or two or three or even four, and they become hooked to the phone as applications. Now students have an arsenal of several new pitches to throw out into cyberspace. They do not have to go to the computer lab to send a nasty email; they can now do it on their lap at their desk when their teacher is . . . well, teaching.

The year is 2006 and that is when the seeds of social media magic or madness really started to take root in society. Fourteen years later or so, you can watch the documentary, *The Social Dilemma* (2020) on Netflix and align the reality to your own experience. But again, for this author, that is the timeline. In the school year 2004–2005, there were no cell phones or just a handful in the school, but not a major pedagogical distraction. They were still a novelty, not a norm.

Then, a study leave took this author out of active teaching for a year. And in 2006–2007, most students had a cell phone, or they were constructing their best arguments for their parents as to why they needed a cell phone, and by the end of that year, there was no going back. Cell phones were in the world permanently. Cell phone plus (+) social media plus (+) limited understanding of the psychology computer and social media designers are employing to grow users and subscribers, and now you have a toxic recipe for social disaster. Whoa, that is harsh. But this author is not the only one writing or thinking about this, and there is ample evidence from 2006 up to the present day. The cycle is going on and on. This chapter is starting to get out of control, just like our social world, so moving to its closure seems prudent. Perhaps it is time for a case study to consider.

The Case of Bartricia (a Pseudonym)

Okay . . . A fictional Grade 11 teacher by the name of Bartricia Schmokey has just returned to the school they left for a year. Bart (as colleagues call Bartricia) had taken a year off to take graduate courses as part of a master's degree requirement. Upon returning to the same school after the year of study,

Bart notices that most students have cell phones in their possession and many are using them without pause in their classes. After a few weeks of trying to engage students, Bart sees clearly that their cell phone use is having an impact on their learning in the classes Bart is teaching. Hmmmm . . . Bart wonders . . . This certainly was not a problem Bart observed a year before the study leave. It seems that rather than following their feet, the students are following their phones (held out in front of them—eyes to the screen) as they walk around the school and even over to the Dairy Queen across the street. In fact, several students were almost hit at a crosswalk because they were not paying attention to traffic.

Concerned, Bart emails the principal and vice principal (two wonderful and wonderfully busy individuals) and suggests a quick meeting to discuss this cell phone usage and to learn if this is actually an issue in the school (As Bart sees it—the overuse and inappropriate cell phone use by students). Or, is this simply an overreaction by Bart? Both the principal and vice principal are very open and approachable.

Bart reflects more . . . is it really an issue? After all, we are in a technological world; we are infusing all types of electronic gadgetry into our schools, classrooms, cars, homes, boats, and watches. There are professional development sessions on SMART Boards, smartphones, and smart-classrooms. Hmmmm . . . Is this cell phone issue really an issue for Grade 11 students and their learning? After all, Bart has noticed that most of the teachers in the school have cell phones. While on break, Bart has noticed some teachers at their desks or in the hallways talking on their phones or sending text messages or checking scores off TSN (The Sports Network in Canada). In the staff room at lunchtime, Bart notices that the usual educational chatter among colleagues is not the same as it was before Bart's study leave. Many colleagues are now on their phones. Bart is dismayed by this reality. Bart is very social and likes to visit at lunch. Now this collegial interaction is not happening in the staff room as it did in previous years.

Bart also notices some teachers have confiscated some cell phones from students. In fact, the school's administrative assistant has several student cell phones on her desk every day, which teachers have dropped off for students to pick up after school. Bart has also noticed that many parents have come in and have been quite angry that their daughter or son had their cell phone taken away for that day because the parent could not communicate with them. Bart heard one parent say, "My other child waited outside her school for two hours because my daughter had her phone taken away and I couldn't send them a message that she was to pick her up!" Is this an issue, Bart wonders again? Perhaps Bart is overreacting. After all, Bart has a cell phone, too.

Bartricia is granted the meeting with the admin team. Bart arrives at the meeting five minutes ahead of schedule and the principal is just finishing up some emails. The vice principal is checking TSN scores on his smartphone. Bart begins to describe the observations and during the meeting, the principal's cell phone goes off twice, interrupting the conversation. The first time, it is the superintendent and the second time it is the principal's partner wondering about their children. Bart continues though and says that teaching and learning may be in a state of erosion in the school as many students are texting each other in class, in other classes, from bathrooms, and between schools. Many of Bart's students are not really that engaged in Shakespearean lessons, poetry, and writing short stories as they once were. Plus, there are reports of cell phone cyberbullying.

"Hmmmm," the principal says, drumming the corner of his cell phone on his desk. There is a long silence . . . Bart is a little frustrated and looks around the room and sees that the vice principal is eyeing his phone after a ping. Forlorn, Bart asks, "Who won the game last night between the Leafs and the Canadiens?"

The Indeterminate Situation

The case study has been incorporated several times since 2015 in one of the author's graduate courses at the University of New Brunswick. The course has been conceptualized and constructed on such leadership practicalities and theories associated with professional supervision, mentoring, and coaching of educators to build their competencies, comfort levels, and confidence for leading. Initially it was a way for the professor to find out what the main conundrums were that educators and school leaders were facing in their schools and communities with technology, but the case kept on evolving.

The case study is loosely based on several educational experiences of the professor when he was a public school educator and has been adjusted from year to year as he learned more about his graduate students. What is conclusive is that cell phones and social media are still the most significant disruptor in schools across Canada, where most of the graduate students are working as they take their master's degree through online delivery. Just as it became the disruptor in and around 2006, cell phone use and social media interaction is disrupting and eroding teaching and learning in schools.

That is a huge claim, no doubt, and the hairs on the back of many readers of this chapter are probably pushing through their clothing. But for now, reflection is needed here. It is acceptable that there will be a huge divide on this issue among school leaders, educators, and especially the students who believe that a contemporary education does in fact involve the cell phone and digital media. There is no intent of casting blame in any direction through this small case study.

The intention of the case study activity for graduate students is to richly describe a contemporary technological dilemma well and comprehensibly and see how they respond. Most go nuts with how the scene or parts of the scene align with their schools and teaching lives. And these are students from across social and political boundaries taking their graduate work together through online learning. Yes, the irony is thick and dramatic. A better research sample could not be provided, really. How does it align with your leading, teaching and learning life? Can you produce another case study that is better than the author's?

If you say that cell phones and social media are not a problem in your life in 2020, that is fine. Design the case study. There is a way to incorporate them positively in pedagogy. But because of the ubiquities attached to social media and cell phones, educators and school leaders must constantly be vigilante on the little or large fires that ignite because of usage. And that takes energy and more learning. And that is social reality in school today. Most definitively, that reality is everywhere.

Mary Aitken's (2017) book *The Cyber Effect* is another excellent resource for educators wanting more information about the internet, and no matter how up to date you are with digital technologies, you will find her ideas very illuminating, stimulating, and perhaps quite frightening, as this author did. The teacher Bartricia in the case study faced an "indeterminate situation" in their teaching that required a leadership response at some level. An indeterminate situation as Biesta and Burbules (2003) write is when

> A teacher may feel uneasy about what is happening in her classroom, and as a result may be distracted or find it difficult to focus. The normal "flow" of teaching is, in a sense, disrupted. For Dewey this would count as an indeterminate situation. As soon as the teacher acknowledges that something needs to be done, that the source of the uneasiness should be identified, the indeterminate situation turns into a problematic situation. It is here that inquiry begins. (p. 58)

Bartricia was looking for support, and instead became frustrated because cell phones had not only taken over the lives of the students in the school but had the attention of staff and school leaders. It is easy to give up in this situation and sadly many teachers do so because they do not want to fight with students over cell phones. They do not want to fight with their parents. But educators cannot give up. This is a fight you must be in fully in 2020 or you will lose many students in many ways and, some deadly. According to the documentarians of *The Social Dilemma*, social media users are under a spell. It is a world of addiction and manipulation. Please watch that show.

November 23, 2020—The Darkness Continues to Rise

"The time is out of joint" (Shakespeare in Evans, 1974). Can it get any worse? On this day, COVID-19 cases are increasing rapidly. Hospitals are filling up across North America and even the places the disease had not claimed due to geographical reasons perhaps, or just pure luck, are seeing terrifying numbers of cases. Winter is now here. The cold and darkness of the north will make it even worse and unbearable for the psychologically vulnerable populations. There will be more lockdowns and that will cause more social unrest. Worst perhaps, the United States election saga continues, and the world awaits a new democratic leader. If we think in dark depths much longer, that will not be good for any one of us. Find hope. Surround yourself with hope. It is the way; it is the only way.

CHAPTER 3 ACTIVITIES AND QUESTIONS

1. When did you write your first email? What was the context you wrote it in? Do you prefer email to social media platforms for communication? Explain.
2. What are advantages to digital communications? What are the disadvantages? Have a roundtable discussion.
3. When did you learn about the Cold War and the potential for global thermonuclear war? Did it cause you anxiety? Please explain.
4. How often does your school or organization practice safety drills like lockdowns? What is it like? Have you ever been in a real lockdown situation? What was it like? How did the leaders, educators, and students respond?
5. In this period of rapid change, what has been your indeterminate or crucible moment that caused you to respond in a productive way in your life? Please elaborate. Share with your classmates.

REFERENCES

Aitken, M. (2017). *The cyber effect.* New York: Spiegel & Grau.

Badham, J. (1983). *WarGames* [Film]. United Artists.

Biesta, G. J. and Burbules, N. C. (2003). *Pragmatism and educational research.* Lanham, MD: Rowman & Littlefield.

Brown, B. (2017). *Braving the wilderness: The quest for true belonging and the courage to strand alone.* New York: Random House.

Bryden, J. (2020, February 25). "That is part of my story now": Trudeau talks about blackface scandal at Black History Month event. *The Canadian Press.* Retrieved from https://nationalpost.com/news/trudeau-revisits-blackface-embarrassment -during-black-history-month.

Fukuyama, F. (1993). *The end of history and the last man.* New York: Simon & Schuster.

Gleick, J. (1999). *Faster.* New York: Vintage Books, Random House.

Graff, G. (2017). *Raven rock.* New York: Simon & Schuster.

Hinton, S. E. (1967). *The outsiders.* New York: Viking Press.

Miranda, L. (2020, October 30). Walmart reverses decision to remove guns and ammo from store shelves. *NBC News Online*. Retrieved from https://www.nbcnews .com/business/consumer/walmart-reverses-decision-remove-guns-ammo-store -shelves-n1245518.

Orlowski, J. (2020). *The social dilemma* [film]. Netflix.

Shakespeare, W. In Evans, G. B. (1974). *The riverside Shakespeare*. Boston: Houghton Mifflin.

Wallerstein, I. (2005). *World-systems analysis: An introduction.* Durham, NC: Duke University Press.

Chapter 4

Bleeding Hearts and Butchers

The Grade 4 teacher was constantly checking her news feed circuit on her cell phone for the election results. The bell would ring any moment and her students would begin entering the building, leaving their play areas for the line-up where they would have their hands sanitized before entering the school. One headline read, "Wait of The World" while another stated, "Election Too Close to Call." She had tried to eat breakfast that morning, but nothing seemed palatable for Ms. Hamilton.

The day before on her drive home, she watched in horror and fascination as business owners in the nation's capital city applied heavy plywood barriers and stabilized them with 2 by 4 long boards over their store windows. The major department stores had been doing the same on the weekend leading up to the election, but small business owners could not afford to do it until the last minute. They could not afford to lose any more business.

The first wave of the COVID-19 pandemic had closed their businesses; they were only now beginning to catch up economically. Broken windows, stolen merchandise, and more disruption would put many on the edge of permanent closure. Ms. Hamilton noticed that many small businesses were going to take the chance by not boarding up.

From a distance, she could hear students entering the hallway. She put her phone in her desk, raised her mask over her nose, and went outside her classroom to greet the students. Inside and sanitized, the children were giggling, pushing, and arguing as they made their way to their lockers to place their belongings and store their lunches. Several teachers who were at their doors were telling children to lift their masks up over their noses. Several did and some did not. The organized children were quick to the teacher's door.

"Good morning Ms. Hamilton," one boy said as he hugged his teacher. Two other teachers stared in shock and disbelief at her. The little boy needed a hug every morning. Ms. Hamilton did not mind showing him affection and paid no attention to the silent reprimands from her colleagues.

She wandered over to Sumeya, a young refugee student who had recently arrived in the United States and had been out of school for two years due to the war that pushed her and her surviving family members out of their country. She was having difficulty with her hijab and face mask at the same time and she was clearly upset. Ms. Hamilton gently put her hand on her shoulder, and the young student turned into her and began crying.

It took a few moments, but Ms. Hamilton's touch and gentleness soothed the child and calmed her down. They could not verbally communicate in English with each other yet, as Sumeya was just going through her initial English as a second language (ESL) class learning. She was making great progress and she trusted her teacher and understood the care in Ms. Hamilton's posture and loving eyes. The teacher straightened out the mask as the young girl pulled on her hijab. They giggled. Together they were able accomplish the task and walked into the classroom.

Ms. Hamilton positioned Sumeya near two other students who spoke Arabic and had a basic grasp on English, at the front of the classroom. In all, Ms. Hamilton had twenty-eight students to teach and lead and fifteen of the children had been born outside the country and were only now learning English. Most English language learners (ELLs) would be in and out of Ms. Hamilton's class each day as they slowly gained competence in the dominant language with their ESL teacher who taught them in another classroom in the school. Each time they left and reentered the classroom, they had to sanitize. Each child was now accustomed to the new norm.

With students now seated in their desks, and nearly five feet apart from each other, Ms. Hamilton gave the signal for everyone to take off their masks and place them in their desk. The children were invited to talk about the morning. One young boy asked, "Ms. Hamilton, is it true there is an island of plastic garbage the size of Texas in the Pacific Ocean?"

Ms. Hamilton's heart sank as she searched for a grade-level response.

SANITIZED SOCIETY

Humans often forget that no matter what life is like in the age/era that they are living in, they are always surrounded and confronted with innocence. In fact, it is the innocence that children bring to their classrooms that inspire their teachers to craft the learning journeys that they aspire to, especially in the younger grades. There is nothing so meaningful for an educator than perceiving a student grasping and holding onto a new concept in their mind and learning how to apply it in real-world contexts.

Ms. Hamilton is teaching and leading Grade 4 children who, for the most part, are still behaving like Grade 4 children, even though they are existentially living in a highly complex period of time in their young lives. They are curious. They are rambunctious. And they are sensitive. And on this day, they are living through a global pandemic where they must follow new social rules and guidelines encouraged and imposed in their communities, on their playgrounds, and inside their classrooms. They are living in a sanitized society.

On this day, November 4, 2020, the students in the scene have many things operating in their world and for much of it they seem oblivious and ambivalent to. Their basic attentions are occupied with being with their friends, being liked, and being able to play. Wearing face masks, rubbing their hands perpetually with an alcohol-based liquid solution, and learning content in their courses are simply things they MUST do in 2020. Most are not yet able to comprehensively consider why such things are necessary. But as the student's question indicates at the end of the vignette, they are starting to awaken to social issues. Innocence still prevails, but only for a short while longer. Like all humans, they will soon run head on into the turbulent social, economic, and environmental conditions in their communities, regions, and countries. In 2020, there is no way to escape any of it. Going off the grid does not even shield people anymore. They are forever connected.

The author is not claiming that children are not learning about social issues before the age of nine or ten and Grades 4 and 5. Many of their teachers are designing lessons about the environment and social group relations as necessary and aimed at their level of understanding. The point here is to unpack what Ms. Hamilton, and thousands and thousands of other educators, are teaching and leading through on this day, November 4, 2020, in this time in our history.

She is following her national election in the United States that has local, national, and global ramifications. The election is over. But then it was not over, as the outgoing president, Donald Trump, continued to rally his political base on the suggestion that the election was rigged. The aftermath of the election further compounded the social upheaval that the entire world was living through. Sanity had not returned, and the ground is still shaking in North America as the author continues to pen his thoughts.

It is apparent that Ms. Hamilton is fearful that civil unrest will break out nearby in the community she serves and that she and her children will be affected by the violence that might follow. She may have to respond to student questions about windows being boarded up and the increased police presence in their neighborhoods later in the day or in the coming weeks. And then, there will be other discussions related to these matters as the election results slowly filter into their realities and leadership from the winner and loser of the election emerges.

Further, Ms. Hamilton is teaching in an ethnocultural diverse educational setting. Quite possibly it is very different from her own K–12 educational experience and certainly it is different from her parents' and grandparents' educational experience in the United States. And if Ms. Hamilton taught in Canada, her experience would parallel that country's ethnocultural and linguistic diversity.

Still further, only illuminated are the ethnocultural, linguistic, and religious differences among the children in her classroom, but there are potentially more aspects of human and social diversity in the classroom that she must address and teach her children about this school year to prepare them for Grade 5 and their increasingly diverse, complex, and turbulent world, outside the ethnocultural qualities of the social setting they are learning in.

Ms. Hamilton's students will soon have questions about gender identity, sexual orientation, and same-gender partnerships, especially if they learn about another student's same-gender parental relationship arrangement. If it is not learned through a structured lesson designed by the teacher, the subject matter will be learned on the playground and will no doubt be twisted and confused by innocent distortion. It is then, sadly, when their minds may become a fertile ground for cruel attitudes and stereotypes about such relationships existing in their worlds.

In Grades 4 and 5, most students have not learned how to exercise the filters in their minds to inquire about such modern family and social realities associated with diversity in its multiple forms. For the prepared educator and leader, it makes teaching fun, meaningful, but extremely challenging which necessitates precise planning. There is no "winging it" in a diverse social context. An educator must be on their game, know their "stuff" cold, and anticipate all types of questions like the one Ms. Hamilton received from the student about the ocean. And they cannot be afraid to be wrong. Further, a diverse educational context can also make teaching terrifying for educators who are afraid that they might cause offense and thus create a flashpoint for themselves. This stuff happens and news cycles are always looking for that educator with the bad lesson that gets on social media platforms.

Next, Ms. Hamilton is greeted with a question about the oceanic environment and some of the major damage humans have bestowed on the planet (and on themselves) the past millennium (Ford, 2020; Ritchie and Roser, 2018; *World Wildlife Magazine*, 2019). We cannot even let the ancient Vikings off the hook here as archaeologists continue to unearth remnants from their past. However, once the industrial revolution took hold, events started to foster rapid social, economic, and environmental change. As evidence, any student can find industrial smokestacks in the social studies textbooks, if they wish to. The industrial world picked up pace, slowly at first, then faster. Now we may be at a point of no return (Attenborough, 2020). Or so it appears if one chooses to follow the scientific discourse on such matters.

A high school teacher might be able to explain to students at that level how humans have butchered their world, because they are working with more mature minds. Fear and anxiety will still be deeply experienced by the high school student, but they have agency to choose to act. Ms. Hamilton cannot tell her Grade 4 students this, at least not in the same way a high school science teacher can introduce the issue and encourage students to investigate and examine it. She cannot even hint at the environmental devastation. Such dialogue at a young age may cause her children to lose hope in their world and many may give up before they really begin their lives.

Instead, she will have to plan her lessons on the environment effectively and at a level where they believe they can make positive change on the planet. She will have to engage them in discussions about climate change and the purpose behind Greta Thunberg's calls for global action. She will have to teach them about the proper methods and actions of recycling waste and plastics to not cause further anxiety and despair for her students. Above all, she must instill within them, hope. And yes, so too does the high school teacher.

And the biggest challenge of all for Ms. Hamilton on this day in this turbulent and tumultuous world is not about an election. It is not about ethnocultural diversity and how to learn about, live with, and get along with people from cultures unlike their own. It is not about climate change and the microplastics in our drinking water and deep inside the fish we consume that are harvested and eaten, either in the wild or from the thousands of aquaculture farming organizations around the world. That is all important. But first, she must help them survive a global pandemic.

HUMAN MOVEMENT AROUND THE WORLD

Across North America, and in many countries around the world, classrooms are becoming similar to Ms. Hamilton's as described in the short scene. They are or they are fast becoming increasingly ethnoculturally, linguistically, and religiously diverse. What was once perhaps a demographically changing human reality more aligned and in step with urban and suburban community development in the United States and Canada (i.e., New York City, Toronto, Vancouver), has gradually shifted to smaller cities and rural regions in North America. The rural towns and regions of North America are becoming settings where new immigrant families can find employment. Many of the newcomers argue that rural communities offer safer schools for their children than what they had experienced in their home country (L. Hamm, Bragdon, McLoughlin, Massfeller & L. A. Hamm, forthcoming).

Societal challenges due to war, poverty, and lack of opportunity are driving millions of people to seek safety outside their original homelands. It is important to reiterate this social reality because it is one that will challenge teachers in the future. People want to come to North America, just as they did the past few centuries. That trending demographic change across much of the world will only heighten as countries such as Canada and the United States fuel and expand their primary, secondary and tertiary-level industrial sectors and continue to advance their technological sectors related to new energy development, artificial intelligence, and cyber security, as prime examples.

But where cities were once the chosen destination for new immigrants, it is now the country or rural landscapes. Set up the factories, meat plants, and industries near the resources, and they will come, right? Cut down on transportation costs. Besides, it is much more affordable to live in a smaller community than a larger one in the current real estate market. Check it out.

People are coming to North America as fast as they came in the late nineteenth and early twentieth centuries. Eerily like those times, thousands are escaping the butchery of war, the cruel totalitarian leadership in their countries, drug cartels, and refugee camps. Ms. Hamilton may symbolize a twenty-first-century educator and stand as one educator who has responded effectively to the new global realities by virtue of her caring nature.

However, most educators in North America are not at all prepared to respond to the daily challenges of ethnocultural and social diversity in their classrooms and the new realities cause them dread and anxiety. How do you teach a child who has lived in a shipping container for a year? In a refugee camp for four years? Painting this picture in general terms will generate opposition from many social directions, but it is no stretch to say that educators require more professional support and learning to keep up with the needs that their students, and many of their family members who will rely on the school for their adjustment, present to them in 2020 and beyond.

The scope of these matters is wide, and this chapter can only braze the surface of the complexity associated to rapid ethnocultural demographic changes brought on by the factors described above. Consider the following case excerpt and think about how you might respond in the situation.

"Mr. Hart, I Have Seen a Lot of Dead People"

When Sam entered Mr. Hart's Grade 8 classroom, the girls could not take their eyes off him. No matter how the teacher tried to gain their attention back to his junior high social studies lessons, their attentions were squarely focused on Sam's soft demeanor, gentle presence, and extremely handsome appearance. Early in the year, it was entertaining to watch how oblivious Sam was to the adolescent turbulence he was creating. He sat quietly and said very little, while focusing on his learning in meticulous rhythm at his desk.

When Mr. Hart would circulate and ask students if they needed some help with their assignments, Sam always declined his offer—never wishing for extra attention on him. When Mr. Hart would ask him if he understood what was being addressed in the curriculum, he would affirmatively nod or say "yes" and yet Mr. Hart was concerned about his grasp on Canadian history.

In this class, English was the first language for 70 percent of the students in a class of twenty-eight. Some of the history lessons focused on immigration to Canada and settlement patterns across the country. Mr. Hart tried to engage students about their family histories and encourage them to investigate their connection to Canada—the struggles, the successes, and the celebrations and life pattern trajectories they knew of and could learn more of through interviewing family members. Understandably, the new immigrant and refugee students in the class hesitated with this assignment for many reasons and yet, Mr. Hart encouraged them throughout the process to apply all the efforts that they could using the educational capital they had.

Sam sat there and reflected on his assignment. Mr. Hart had a sense of what he and his family had been through in their homeland and on their journey to Canada and into the community. Teachers were on a need-to-know basis from school administration and what had happened to Sam and his family wasn't shared with anyone at that point.

As the project was nearing its conclusion, students were busily completing the final stages, Sam sat at his desk with a few pieces of paper that he would shuffle around. It was clear he was considering the assignment; it was clear he wanted to complete it. When asked if he required extra time, he gently said, "No thank you. I am fine."

Near the end of class the following day, he asked, "Mr. Hart, can I stay after school so you can help me with my assignment?" Finally, a chance to visit with him, and to learn how he could support him. The teacher agreed and moved the class to its closure. The students cleared for their next class and at the end of that day, Sam arrived with his work in hand. He placed his binder on his desk, looked at his teacher, and said matter-of-factly, "Mr. Hart, a rocket hit our house." There was moment of silence and Mr. Hart echoed his question. "A rocket hit your house?"

"Yes Mr. Hart. Should I tell that story about my family?"

"Can you tell me a little bit more?"

"We were woken up by the alarms; we got dressed fast. We got into the car and we were driving away really, really fast. When I looked back, I saw the rocket hit our house. It started a big fire."

For the next hour or so, they worked on the project and shared stories. They both listened carefully to each other and became sealed in dialogue. The teacher as student; the student as teacher. Admittedly, there were moments that Mr. Hart wanted to cry. But he did not.

"Mr. Hart. I have seen a lot of dead people."

"I know."

Here Comes Everyone

Since the 1990s, political and societal conflicts in many countries have left millions of people homeless, dead, or on the move around the planet, chased by the existential horror of the modern-day reality of war. It is on television, on radio, in the newspapers. War is always present in 2020 somewhere whether it makes the front page, back page, or no page. Many children and their families live it firsthand outside of North America.

Since 2000, Europe and North America have been destinations of choice for thousands of people. Many have no choice. The conflicts that continue to rage in 2020 show no signs of letting up and the people will continue to arrive in countries like Canada and the United States where they will not speak the dominant language (in Canada, it is English and French), nor will they understand the laws or cultural values of its citizenry, and many will unfortunately face multiple forms of social and prejudicial resistance, marginalization, and injustice due to their "otherly" presence in their new communities.

Much has been written on this contemporary reality through academic research and professional literature and this author has tried his best to contribute to the conversation by exposing the realities, the responses, and the hope and dreams of newcomers. In one province in Canada, the Alberta Teachers' Association responded a few years ago by creating a teaching document for its professional and paraprofessional staff called *Here Comes Everyone: Teaching in the Intercultural Classroom* (2010) after leaders within that provincial teachers' association identified how the rapid demographic changes were impacting its educators.

Yet, no matter what has been written, presented at conferences, in webinars, and at school and district professional development sessions, or posted through blogs and Facebook connections, it all comes down to how frontline educators like Ms. Hamilton and Mr. Hart will respond to the challenges that their students present them or as they require their teachers to go beyond their professional call of duty.

They will have to decide how they will respond to the daily complexities they encounter in their service and leadership for each of their students, but especially for those students, like Sumeya and Sam, who left everything behind, not because they wanted to, but because they had to. They will require empathy, compassion, and patience from their teachers if they are to have any chance of realizing their dreams in North America.

PROGRESS—THE PARADOX OF PAYING FOR SINS OF HISTORY

Have you ever found yourself somewhere in North America, driving down a highway with beauty surrounding you? Suddenly, you are confronted with the real sign of severe human interaction with the observable natural environment. It could be a large clear-cut forest. Or a barren landscape of tailing pond externalities from a mine or mill located in the area. A graveyard of commercial airliners no longer in service, rusting and disintegrating slowly back into the earth. It could even be an abandoned oil pump-jack or several that dot the rolling horizon.

All these environmental realities could result in fewer and fewer fish in lakes, rivers, and streams—fewer wild animals in the woods or on the great plains of North America. Poisoned oxygen and less healthy space for humans. Pick an industry near you. It is maddening. It is saddening. But it is human progress. It is the cruel paradox of our times.

It is not the author's intention to take a stab at the workplaces that provide people their jobs, security, and livelihoods and allow their families in the new millennium to survive. But he has. In fact, this writer would not be doing what he is doing professionally if it were not for the generous employment opportunities he received from mining and petroleum industries to help him pay for his tuition when he was younger.

It is, however, important to unpack the question the young boy posed to Ms. Hamilton about all the plastic and garbage floating in the ocean because that is his world and he will need to know how to deal with all the damage (https://www.nationalgeographic.org/encyclopedia/great-pacific-garbage-patch/). For the reflective educator and leader, it must seem a real tragedy that it is the children they are leading that are going to pay for the sins of history and progress as we all do. They are going to suffer in a big, big way. But there is hope.

Necessity is the mother of invention, and right now, the world needs the tools to undo what has been done. But to throw more fuel to this burning fire will do nothing more than add to the million of loud voices already in this conversation. Loud, because they are screaming and the world keeps rolling, and many people are not really paying much attention.

What educators and their students need now is something solid to work with, that goes beyond conceptualization and the local actions more schools have mandated. Recycle your paper, cans, and bottles. Clean up your school yards and communities. Bring your own water bottles. These are great ideas from the past quarter century, but the impact they are having really needs to be examined as the engines of industry keep pushing forth.

A teacher and their students need only do a Google search of the ocean and plastics to discover environmental horror and devastation. Several solid resources have been added at the end of this chapter in the references. They do not have to see the devastation firsthand by traveling across the country or taking a cruise ship vacation. The visual devastation is at their fingertips.

As the world keeps warming up, our ice caps at the top and bottom of our planet are melting; low lying areas will flood and push millions more people from their homelands. This is all known and in the news most days each week when elections and pandemics are not preoccupying the attentions of viewers. Ms. Hamilton, what is your strategy on this day? How will you respond to the question? Will it alleviate the anxiety that your students are feeling, but not yet fully comprehending? There is an opportunity for leadership growth in your students. Harness their energies, give them hope, and challenge them to run toward the problems with plastics. Otherwise, they may run away and hide from the problems that face them.

NOVEMBER 28, 2020: WHEN WILL THIS END? WILL IT END?

It is nearly four weeks later, and Ms. Hamilton is not sure what will happen at the White House. Each day her students in her class bicker about who won the election. Several side with one candidate; several side with the other. "My dad says . . . my mom says . . . my grandpa says . . ." On the playground, there have been fights among several students and teachers and support staff have intervened. In the staff room, several colleagues are at odds with each other. Some believe the election was fair; some suggest that there was mischief somewhere. They walk away from each other. There is social unrest. The school is a microcosm. The school is the human laboratory.

Another day, another long line of sanitation? COVID-19 is raging, raging, raging. Thank you, essential service providers. Wear a mask. Do not wear a mask. Take your grievance to the streets. Take your grievance online. Ms. Hamilton is confused. She is tired at the end of November. Christmas break is still three weeks away. She cannot see her family. Her dad is not well. She will not get to hold him this Christmas. Her heart is bleeding. When will the social butchery end? Will it ever? It must.

CHAPTER 4 ACTIVITIES AND QUESTIONS

1. If you were Ms. Hamilton's school leader, how would you provide her hope and inspiration during COVID-19?
2. What are some of the projects you have had your students address related to plastics and community waste?

REFERENCES

Alberta Teachers' Association (2010). *Here comes everyone: Teaching in the intercultural classroom.* Retrieved from https://www.teachers.ab.ca/sitecollection-documents/ata/publications/human-rights-issues/mon-3%20here%20comes%20everyone.pdf.

Attenborough, D. (2020). *A life on our planet: My witness statement and a vision for the future.* New York: Grand Central Publishing.

Ford, D. (2020). COVID-19 has worsened the ocean plastic pollution problem. A drastic increase in use of masks and gloves, plus a decline in recycling programs, is threatening the health of seas. *Scientific American.* Retrieved from https://www.scientificamerican.com/article/covid-19-has-worsened-the-ocean-plastic-pollution-problem/.

Hamm, L., Bragdon, McLoughlin, Massfeller, L. A. Hamm. (Forthcoming). Diversity, growth, and understanding: School responses to immigration in rural New Brunswick. *Canadian journal of educational administration and policy.*

Ritchie, H. and Roser, M. (2018). Plastic pollution. Published online at *OurWorldInData.org.* Retrieved from https://ourworldindata.org/plastic-pollution [Online Resource].

World Wildlife Magazine. (2019, Fall). Plastic in the ocean: Plastic waste is flooding our oceans. It's more important than ever to reduce our plastic footprint worldwide. Retrieved from https://www.worldwildlife.org/magazine/issues/fall-2019/articles/plastic-in-the-ocean.

Chapter 5

From Darkness to Light

The student was unhappy. As the teacher was finishing the lesson with his final comments, she pondered what she had learned. Certainly, her teacher's selection of poetry, essays, and short stories were interesting and engaging in this unit as in previous ones, but they lacked something that was very important for her, and at the moment, she couldn't figure out what that was. She was not one to confront her teachers, but something was compelling her to speak now.

She pretended to organize her binder as her peers left the classroom. It was the ten-minute break, so she knew she had ample time to get to her next class. The teacher was tidying up his overhead transparencies, getting them ready for his next class, which was another section of Grade 9 English. With borrowed courage, she pulled her mask up over her nose, and approached him. He looked up.

> "Hey, what's up, Jen? You might be late for your next class, so you should hurry."

> "I have time Mr. Hernandez. I was wondering about the lesson today. It was really . . . well . . . rather frightening, especially with everything going on in the world right now."

"Frightening?" The teacher reflected for a moment. The poem was called "Five Ways to Kill a Man." He quickly reached back into his mind for the rationale behind his poetic selection, something he had not written down on his daily plan, but he had taught this poem before. Not every year, but several times during his career up to this point. He looked into her eyes and now wondered if other students were feeling the same. He could feel his heart rate accelerate.

Instantaneously, his mind played back the lesson from the start. There was a great discussion during the class; most students seemed engaged; they could figure out the historical puzzle in each stanza; they understood the main theme. There definitely was comprehension, which was important going into the English achievement test.

He was more at ease and asked, "What was frightening, Jen? I mean, that was the point . . . in another way . . . to show students that humans have not been nice to humans throughout history. There have been social conundrums all along the course of history. It's not just happening today in our time. It was just a literary example. We will get through all of this, Jen." He tried to be reassuring, as he always did.

But reassuring was not enough. The student nodded throughout the teacher's explanation. When he was finished, she paused to collect her thoughts.

"Mr. H., in the last twenty years, planes have flown into buildings, there are wars everywhere, the ice caps are melting, my friends are hating each other on social media, and now we have to wear masks in school."

"I know that Jen. I am hoping that students will rise to the challenges of their world and find the solutions that humans need. And of course, we all must learn to be kind to each other."

Then her eyes widened in realization of what was missing from Mr. Hernandez's lessons in this unit.

"Yes Mr. H., but we can't do any of that without hope. We need to hope. We cannot lose hope. We need it now more than ever."

MOVE BEYOND JUST HOPING

In many jurisdictions across North America, English teachers have full or near-full autonomy to choose what they teach as long as they challenge their students with a balanced literacy and writing program. Math, social studies, history, and science teachers generally have a leveled curriculum that they must learn, plan, and teach their students throughout the school year, generally separated into larger units or sections. Jurisdictions are not the same from province to province or state to state, as reading lists, history subjects, science topics, and math expectations vary with suggested age-appropriate selections from district or government curriculum leaders. When governments change, curricula changes. Curriculum is highly political.

But English teachers have the opportunity to craft and recraft their learning programs from year to year. Many of these educators look for opportunities to connect engaging current events to their selections of poems, songs, novels, plays, and essays in their units, which are often thematically and loosely strung together. This pedagogical approach is an attempt to increase student engagement and help students build critical thinking skills.

A strong educator first gets to know their students and then finds what they are interested in as part of their balanced programming while infusing engaging lessons along the way. There is a plan, but the plan must be flexible, given the reality of just how rapid the world, and the social contexts of student lives, are accelerating and changing.

Math, science, history, and social studies educators work their craft to build critical thinking skills in students also, and the strong teachers are the ones who go outside the mandated curriculum outcomes for student learning and bridge their students to their natural and human-constructed worlds. It is a claim based on thirty years in education as a classroom teacher, administrator who supervised all the subject areas in two Canadian provinces, and now in service as an associate professor who teaches teachers and school leaders. If math, science, social studies, and English teachers dispute this, then the author welcomes their input. He is never finished learning.

But that is not the point at this moment at the start of the chapter. The question is, at what age are students fully ready to learn about events in the world—those from the past, and in the present? At what age are they ready to learn about the complex and turbulence in their lives to prepare them for a world that really cannot be comprehended. And 2020 has left humans that lesson forever.

In the English literature world, there are all types of interesting, heroic, and nasty characters to learn about, to satisfy a creative and curious learning spirit in every student. After common literary elements of setting, plot, rhyme scheme, stanza, and conflict are introduced to students, an astute literature teacher (assuming this is part of the reading lessons in countries outside the English world) begins to introduce the concept of character and characterization into lessons. There is a scaffolding sequence in the teaching and learning, and granted, it will not be the same for every teacher in every province, state, and country.

Then, when an English or literature teacher writes character and characterization on the chalkboard or whiteboard or shows a PowerPoint slide, students really start to pay attention because now they start learning about motives and motivation behind the actions of characters in the story that propel the plot on its course. Is a character round (not fat) with many character traits and psychological qualities? Are they a flat character with few qualities? Are they static in a story and stay the same or are they dynamic and change throughout the tale? And if they are dynamic, what events in the story caused them to change?

And characterization, well . . . that is a heavy concept for students to grasp, especially in the middle years (Grades 5–9 or so). Is the writer directly characterizing a character by telling the reader what they are like, or are they indirectly characterizing a character by describing a character through another character? Oh wow, now a literature class discussion can get interesting beyond the story at hand, because at some time in everyone's life, people talk about other people and sometimes, it really is not that nice. Especially when it is on social media. Nor is it usually fully true, but only true in the perceptions of the speaker. That is true. Or is it? Now the class is investigating the concept of multiple realities that intersect everywhere in the world. Whoa . . . slow down a bit here, writer. What about Jen and Mr. Hernandez?

In Edwin Brock's poem "Five Ways to Kill a Man," the writer takes the reader through a historical look at human inhumanity. At one time, it was thematically coined Man's Inhumanity to Man, but that is now politically incorrect in 2020. The first stanza describes Jesus Christ's crucifixion. The second looks at how knights battled other knights and nobles during the Middle or Dark Ages. The third stanza brings the reader up to World War I and chemical warfare, and the fourth stanza, yes you get it, is about World War II, Adolf Hitler, and the atomic bomb.

But none of those stanzas bother students in Grade 9 and they were not the lines that encouraged Jen to approach her teacher. Most middle school students have heard or learned to some degree the historical events related to each of these periods of time dating back 2,000 years. In fact, if students are reading about the rise of Greek civilization, Homer's *Iliad* and *The Odyssey*, Socrates, Plato, and Aristotle, their learning transcends the story of Jesus, Mary, and Joseph. Just another point to hammer the nail home.

By the age of fourteen, most students in North America know who Brad Pitt is (or Jennifer Aniston, and they can make the connection) and many have watched the movie *Troy* and seen Odysseus's great wooden horse fool the Trojans. That time was about 3,200 years ago. After Googling it, today's students might tell their English teacher that they would never fall for something like that.

Jen was concerned about the last stanza and particularly the last four words in the last line, "and leave him there." Mr. Hernandez had his own interpretation of the narrator, the theme, and those last four words. That was, the world in the first two decades of the twenty-first century was just as dangerous than it had ever been in history. But Jen suggested it was even more dangerous.

It is more dangerous than the times of Romans who conquered and lost the ancient world. It is more dangerous than the world of knights, Robin Hood, King Arthur, and the Black Plague. It is even more dangerous than all the wars combined in the twentieth century and all the nasty characters who were motivated in some way to destroy people, places, and the collective human spirit. Reader, if you look around carefully at the global picture today, you might just agree with Jen.

Jen was fourteen years old and she simply wished that her English teacher would end his lessons with hope—possibility. Inspiration. And more possibility. She did not want to wear a mask in school like all her classmates. She did not want to sanitize every time she entered and left a room in the school or in any of the stores in her community—at least those that have not been locked down.

Point well taken by Mr. Hernandez. You are right, Jen. The world is a mess. It is tumultuous and turbulent and there appears to be no let up in sight. But you are fourteen and you need to believe that there will be light from the darkness and so Mr. Hernandez, you need to really consider the poems you select; the plays you teach, and the songs that you share in the classroom to weave your thematic magical lessons through your units. Darkness must yield to light. There is no other way forward. If 2020 has taught humankind anything, it is that. We need hope. We need peace. The book must end on that.

There is no way to sugarcoat these tumultuous, complex, and turbulent times. People walk around like zombies with headphones on; they watch violence on television or stream it on their smartphone while riding a bus or walking down a street with their dog. This is an age where it seems for many that it is more important to go viral on the internet, than sit down with a neighbor (even at a safe social distance) and talk about the events in the community. Or they may discuss how their sons and daughters are doing in school, about that crazy teacher who set off all the water sprinklers in the school while demonstrating a chemical reaction in the science lab.

Cyberbullying is at an all-time high in 2020 (Aitken, 2017); anxiety and depression are rampant in our student populations, and among educators and school leaders. Racism, inequity, and social media vitriol is taking over the collective consciousness of humanity. The turbulence is stealing human souls. And, sadly, the information age has placed humanity in the disinformation age where people group together on ideology and scream, text, and post their truths at many other groups (Orlowski, 2020). Who is right? Who knows? Who is wrong? Perhaps everyone is complicit in some way in 2020.

SO, WHAT CAN YOU DO TEACHER,
LEADER, AND STUDENT?

There is much that can be done, but what must be done, must be done collectively. That sentence is weird, but it works. No one person can do everything given the state that humans find themselves in today. That is fantastic because this book is about schools, learning and leading communities, teachers, school leaders, students, support staff, parents, and school volunteers who all belong in a school somewhere, who all belong in a community somewhere, who all belong in a country somewhere. They belong. And if there are those who feel like they do not belong, that is a problem, and it must be fixed. In 2020 and afterward, you need everyone on board now.

The school environment, all school environments across North America and all over the world, are the best places for what must be done, to begin. At least to begin again. Because people will have to begin again after they come through this current COVID-19 pandemic. They will begin again. And in this short space of a few chapters, this book has only been able to present and examine a few of the realities that contribute to the rapid changes in our world, and of all times, 2020 will be known henceforth as one of the most challenging years for educators and students in the history of education.

Jen said it best in her statement to her teacher: "Mr. H., in the last 20 years, planes have flown into buildings, there are wars everywhere, the ice caps are melting, my friends are hating each other on social media, and now we have to wear masks in school." Rise, rise from the ashes, young phoenix. You need your school leaders and teachers; they need you. It is time to return to the question: In a world that appears to be coming apart, how should educators in North America, that is, classroom teachers and school administrators who are in formal leadership positions, help their students understand and prepare for such troubling and turbulent times? *What actions can and must they take to counter the confusion and complexity?*

The internet, social media, global wars, migration, immigration, demographic change, and technological advances are perceived conundrums that humans need to get control of. Of course, there are even more serious issues like environmental destruction and disaster that must be tackled immediately (Attenborough, 2020). That is a strong list of turbulent conditions swirling about society, interacting in all sorts of ways, and causing all types of anxieties for people everywhere.

Paradoxically, one cannot look at the list and see just the negative without looking hard for some positives. The internet and social media are damaging in so many ways. Humans from all worldviews and persuasions know this. Yet, the internet and social media allow people to connect and communicate with each other during a pandemic. The multiple platforms allow friends to reengage each other after many years. It allows sons and daughters to locate their birth fathers and mothers.

Ethnocultural demographic change impacts communities, provinces, and states and often ignites flash points for racism, hatred, and discrimination for people entering a country. But the rapid changes also bring qualified and skilled people together from different parts of the world and fills multiple needs in a society. Think of places in North America that require more workers, doctors, and lawyers, more taxpayers to keep aging infrastructures intact and functional, roads maintained, hospitals and senior citizen complexes fully staffed.

Technological and chemical warfare are just damn awful, with their advanced radar and lasers that destroy battlefield targets and humans in the theater of war. Yet lasers are also used by doctors to destroy cancer cells in their patients. Humans must learn to survive their paradoxes (The Tragically Hip, 1996). Life in 2020 is paradox.

No one sets out to write a thin book. Yet, what must be said here and now has been said before, in some way, somewhere, to some one. It must be said again because it appears no one is really listening. Just watch the news in 2020. People are screaming at each other, carrying a sign of support for this, that, and the other. And they are facing off against a person with a different sign of support—a different point of view. It is terrible. Humans are in an age where instead of talking, they are typing, texting, posting, or tagging (yes, reader, that was stated before). But they are not communicating.

Slowly, society is eroding to a state where no one is living a shared reality, but instead living in time where two people may stand across from each with the number 6 between them. One of them sees a six (6); one sees a nine (9) (LensShift, 2018). Their realities are two numbers apart. Worlds apart and they are there right beside each other. This cannot go on much longer; there will be a breaking point. One must hope we have not gone past it yet. People are dying. They are on sidewalks, getting the life squeezed out of them. "I can't breathe!"

Blame the government. Blame the internet. Blame the neighbor. Blame the teacher. Blame the coach who cut you from the team. Sadly in 2020, taking responsibility seems like someone else's responsibility. But that is too much to address in this book. Stick to education. It must be about education. What can school leaders, teachers, students, support staff, and a myriad of others in the community do in 2020 to counteract all this insanity? What must they do? They can do it. They are our last line of defense before a total breakdown of communication in society. Get to work—now! The world needs you.

THERE IS NO SHORT CUT IN 2020 AND BEYOND

A gentle proposition must be put forward. In 2020, most people know what they need to do, or what needs to be done, to help the world get out of this mess. Even just a little bit and really, that is all schools and the people within them can do. They can do a little bit, each day. Each little bit adds up to a lot of change over time. But thinking, then acting, takes effort and most people in 2020 want shortcuts. Leaders, teachers, and their students are no different in this scenario.

Society wants to Google something to find out more about it; they want to click a button and have supper delivered; they want a car nearby to take them somewhere at a reasonable cost. They want convenience. They want easy street. They want a map. They want to be told what to do so they do not have to figure it out for themselves. Educators are guilty of this in many, many ways. A problem student? "Come in and show me how to work with this student." A new curriculum? "Come in and show me how to teach it."

Sadly, many educators reach a point in their career where it seems they stop learning or prevent themselves from learning through shortcuts. And should not learning be lifelong? Especially for teachers? There are no shortcuts and taking one in 2020 will only invite despair.

So, based on what has been said thus far, a few modest propositions will be put forth with . . . encouragement. Yes, encouragement from an encourager. What that means is that readers are encouraged to consider these few humble suggestions and any of the details, cases, or short vignettes employed to simply add another idea or two to the suggestion.

Strategies is a tough word in 2020 because as everyone knows, contexts matter and what is suggested for one school may not work in another school with another group of educators or students. Just glean an idea or two from each suggestion and consider if it might illuminate a new way or consideration for you to do education or leadership or learning. As Stephen King described in his book *On Writing* (2010), if you take an idea and jam it into a totally different idea, then something marvelous may come out of the interaction. Let us begin. Let everyone begin again.

1. Interrogate Contemporary Communication Before Society Breaks

Get rid of the cell phones. Oh boy, no one wanted to hear that. Okay, please consider a new teaching and learning reality with no cell phones in the classroom. "What about a possible intruder in the school!?" Hmmm, that question was bound to arise. Okay, pick from any of the communication technologies at the disposal of the educator and go with one as an intervention tool for that potential moment of danger. Zoom, Teams, Google Hangouts all stand out at this moment. But kindly stand down Sony, Apple, and Samsung! This does not mean get rid of cell phones completely.

Cell phones, smartphones, wrist phones, headphones, and hip bones (er, phones) are fantastic inventions, and especially when one is driving or walking through (and running from) a snowstorm, tornado, or hurricane somewhere in the world. Oh yes, an immediate safety feature at one's fingertips when none really existed twenty-five years ago, in the current form at least.

Again, this book is about schools, teaching, and learning and cell phones do not belong in the classroom. In any classroom, anywhere. And the evidence is thick for this proposition. This author is relying on fifteen years of experience, observation, and conversation to make this bold statement, not on academic arguments. There can be no living paradox here. Students do not need cell phones in classes. Teachers do not need them in their teaching.

Yes, teachers and students use them, and it looks cool. You can do quizzes on them. Teachers time their lessons with them; they listen to the beeps, blips, and interesting notifications and then they move on. Or they do not, but instead check scores or their email. That is stealing time from teaching and learning.

This is insane, you cannot take cell phones out of schools! Reader, that was not suggested. Take them out of classrooms. Just the classrooms. Just out of the attention range of students for the length of their class so they can concentrate on a big idea. Sixty minutes, fifty minutes, forty minutes. Lord Almighty . . . Twenty minutes! Just long enough for the teacher and students to teach and learn something! To build authenticity in human form, not through artificial form.

The cell phones are going to be in schools. Everyone will have a cell phone. That is the world we now know. Again, take them out of the attention range of students so they can become learners again in the twenty-first century. When a phone beeps, blips, and notifies them, their mind is on the message. So is the teacher's mind. And like Bartricia found out, so is the administrator's mind.

Author, are cell phones not part of twenty-first century learning? Can the question be asked like that? Try again. Are cell phones synonymous with the vision of twenty-first century learning? I do not think that this can be argued. Yes, most certainly. Here's the clincher . . . the students are already ahead of the learning curve an hour after they get their first cell phone.

Their phone is in their hands before breakfast; it is in their hands on the way to school; it is in their hands at lunchtime; it is in their hands after school; it is in their hands at the supper table; it is in their hands while they do their homework; and it is in their hands when they go to bed. It is there beside them on the bed or on the desk when they wake up.

My goodness, do you REALLY believe that students need their cell phones for the four to six hours that they are learning in their classrooms? C'mon! Take back some control school leaders and teachers. Be firm here. Leaders and educators, you MUST show moral courage on this issue (Shields, 2018).

And educators, what really is the message that you are sending children these days when you tell them that you need your cell phone in your classroom, or in your pocket, or on your hip, when you are teaching them? Do you want to go down the street of hypocrisy with middle school students? "Why should the teacher use their cell phone and we cannot use ours? It's hypocrisy,

I say," shouts the student. But really, it is wasted seconds and minutes from teaching and learning through meaningless conflict. The cell phone is a relationship-killer in the classroom. Enough on that.

Now briefly the other side. The teacher who has established a solid relationship with a group of students, has gone over the norms with cell phone usage in their classroom, and believes they have everything under control. Good for you, but sadly, you do not have control. If you are teaching a high school course for approximately 100 hours over the duration of a high school semester, and you and your students are constantly addressing notifications that come through on your phone, what is the teaching and learning time lost? Be mindful of that and run a little study. Add the numbers up. You would be surprised.

Oh, you do not check every notification. But you just received a beep, blip, or buzzing vibration in your pocket? Are you thinking about that notification? If you are, you are now not thinking about teaching or learning. Your normal flow of teaching has been disrupted (Biesta & Burbules, 2003). That is time stolen from children, also. And it cannot be helped because it is built into the software design to get more users through advertisements (Orlowski, 2020).

After fifteen years, educators have had enough time to understand cell phones and the impact they have on teaching and learning. But it has not been a fair fight, and they are no further ahead in 2020 than they were in 2005 when cell phones became more and more apparent and visible in the lives of students. Educators in one Canadian province are on record stating:

> Attention spans are much lower. I would attribute this to technology and constant access to stimulators . . . The emergence of electronic devices have become a grand distraction for many students . . . Across the board in different schools, smart phones have been the primary change throughout my teaching career. Students can no longer focus on task when they are distracted so easily. (L. Hamm, Massfeller, McLoughlin, Bragdon, and L. A. Hamm, 2020, Survey Respondents 22, 24, and 34)

Is it really a far cry to suggest that this would be a common reality in most schools in North America?

Please, please consider taking the cell phones out of your classrooms, out of your everyday pedagogy. There are many more reasons to do this that can be described here, and to be sure, every teacher in 2020 from at least Grade 5 on up has had at least one battle with a student over their cell phone. What does that finding further reveal?

If this part of the chapter seems too contentious, so be it. It is only a suggestion and perhaps the humble suggestion will illustrate the importance of having important conversations about how students use their cell phones. What is appropriate usage; what is inappropriate usage?

And one final point . . . educators, you have so many other electronic and digital tools that you can infuse into your lessons (i.e., SMART Board technology), but the best tool is your mind and learning spirit. Use them to get to know your students; to build relationships with them; to challenge them; and to keep them in conversations. Do not lose them to their cell phones, the internet, and social media. Too many children have been lost already and many more of them will be too difficult to get back. Just watch the news.

2. Keep Schools Open Longer as Public Community Spaces

When the idea for this book was conceived, a global pandemic was not factored into the forecast, the thinking, the writing, and a writer can only stay on defense for so long. Staying on defense is not really part of a writer's DNA. That said, this next suggestion must be based on getting through, over, and beyond COVID-19 and humans will prevail.

At this writing on November 29, 2020, there are already several vaccine companies vying for top spot and several are in the process of getting their medicine cleared by governments for mass implementation. As stated earlier, this book cannot be taken over by COVID-19. The virus is just another tough challenge for school leaders, educators, students, and families in 2020 and will be with them for a while longer. It has been devastating at so many social, psychological, and economic levels and cannot be downplayed. It is devastating. But humans will prevail. Humans collectively are resilient. There is no plan B worth even thinking about.

The question of the day is how will people be able to come together in the future and start communicating more effectively, more openly and honestly, and perhaps learn about another human being who is much, much different from them? Different in their belief systems and worldview; different in color; different in the gods they worship (or do not worship); different in the language they speak; different in sexual preference; just plain different? Because difference seems to be staring down and scaring people more than ever and there are common reasons why.

People are living in crowded cities, and towns (yes, even towns). They are in proximity. People are emigrating from their homes to new and foreign lands and they are experiencing cultural conflict. People are in perpetual contact with people from around the world through their digital media fixation and that type of communication can be fragmenting at best. People are choosing to watch one-sided newscasts to affirm or even confirm the stereotypes in their minds, and that can be dangerous. The reasons for miscommunication and disinformation are endless in 2020.

People need to be in a heart-to-heart setting, with nothing in front of them to shield or protect them. People must come out from behind their desks, their laptops, or their cell phones and face other human beings to learn about and understand each other better. Any school, anywhere, is a wonderful setting for this to occur and most of them are public organizations.

Yet, many schools start up in the morning, and close much too early for people to come together. Our society must rethink schooling and what an education looks like in the future, post-2020. Must students be the only learners in schools? Can the school not be extended to the general community, especially in times of rapid change where people require additional public spaces. To avoid even more digression, a clear path must be set for this part of the suggestion.

The School of the Future

Imagine a school where, after all the children leave for the day, it is now open for the public, until say, midnight. Why that time? Well, ice arenas, bowling alleys, dance studios, coffee shops, and bars and lounges that serve alcohol stay open until approximately that time—some earlier; some later. But unless there is a school sports event after school, most schools close and lock their doors at a regular time.

And then people who do not skate, bowl, dance, or drink coffee and alcohol have few places to go that are free. So, they stay inside and watch people scream at each other on the television or they stream to achieve their discontent on their smart devises. They become idle and being idle is unhealthy physically, socially, and psychologically. They are connected to the world artificially but disconnected from reality authentically. Think about that.

For this author who is arguing about better leadership, learning, and pedagogy during times of rapid change (I had to throw that in there again), the concern becomes real when people from all over the planet start sharing community space and they do not know each other, nor do they take the time to learn about each other.

If there is no common place other than the shopping mall (and most people just walk by each other there), then where is it that people will ever get an opportunity to meet someone else who is different from themselves? Someone who thinks a different way. Someone who votes a different way. Someone who worships a different way. Someone who eats different food. Speaks a different language. Wears different attire.

There seems to be no common public place for humans to come together anymore and learn about each other in a way that will help them break down their stereotypes, their suspicions, and their fears of someone who is different from them. Here's a case scenario to help bring this thought to one's own conclusion.

Come Out from Behind Your Desk and Technology and Be Heard

A professor in a western Canadian university was teaching a graduate course one summer. His class consisted of nineteen diverse, unbelievably innovative, and energetic students taking their initial graduate courses in their master's degree in educational leadership. After the first couple of days of core learning with his teaching pedal on full throttle, the professor wanted to know how close the students had become, and more importantly, how close he had become with them, and if his team and course culture-building activities were bringing the group together. He knew all their names, what they taught at the schools where they worked, and where they were from originally. Most teachers are migratory creatures and move around a lot. But he didn't really know them deeply, and worse, he knew that they didn't know each other deeply, and because of that, they couldn't extend their learning beyond just the content he had laid out in his course outline.

It was apparent that they were all comfortable talking at their tables with each other and moving around from table to table to work with another group of peers when he asked them to. Really, that is standard compliance in any graduate course. Courtesies are most often displayed, but it is still far from authentic value. The professor needed to get them there.

Feeling confident with the extra layer of protection their table desks and laptops (and cell phones) provided them, they openly and fluently talked in whole class discussions professionally, without much prodding from the prof. Hey, they were in their master's program and the initial honeymoon was still being felt by them.

But many were scared, uncertain, and doubtful and the professor knew it because he had seen it over and over throughout twenty-seven years during his teaching and leadership service in public schools and in higher learning institutions. After their class break on the fourth day, the students entered the class and were astonished that the professor had arranged all the seats in a large, and somewhat jagged circle away from their tables.

It was not truly circular, because space was limited in the room, so he asked students to help him further arrange the chairs, so no one was sitting behind or slightly behind the person next to them.

"I would like you all to show your hearts to the center of the circle. You may say something if you wish to. It is not necessary. Just breathe, have some fun, and be present," the professor said. The discomfort level was intense. He could see their minds turning. Where do I sit? Am I going to have to say something? Will I sound silly? I need something to hold onto.

The professor remained casual and patient and he smiled. His forearms rested on his lap, his heart to the circle. Once everyone was settled, there was dead silence. That was the first for this group as they were very cordial and socially delightful to learn with. The energy had not left them. It was a new kind of energy that they were feeling.

The professor started again with a slight joke to disrupt the tension, just a bit. "Hey, thanks for coming back to our class. You know, I just thought we should slow down a bit and perhaps talk about the first few days of your graduate program, your course projects, and maybe get some feedback from each other." It was innocent, inviting, and reassuring on many levels.

Having participated in many indigenous talking circles, the professor had learned that once the heart is open, and free to speak, and there are no digital tools to grasp, everyone has an opportunity to be heard. Truth emerges. One by one, the students spoke about their fluctuating levels of confidence, the doubts that they were wrestling with being in a master's program, and the struggles in their professional and personal lives that had brought them to this moment and to the circle that day.

They heard each other and the generous invitations to gain support and friendship over the next two years in the cohort. They spoke about inequities in their schools that they wanted to address. They learned about the challenges many of their colleagues confronted with prejudice, racism, and discrimination. They learned about each others' hopes and dreams. That day in the circle, they implicitly made a commitment to struggle and learn together. But it would never have been possible until they learned deeply about each other while facing each other directly, with heart open, in the circle.

Enlarge Your Capacity to Lead, Teach, and Learn

One of the best philosophers of our time is Parker Palmer. If you have not read his book *The Courage to Teach*, then you are strongly encouraged to do so, especially when you have time during a global pandemic. He says, "The pace of change has us snarled in complexities, confusions, and conflicts that will diminish us, or do us in, if we do not enlarge our capacity to teach and to learn" (2007, p. 3). Learning should never be one-sided; that is, a person cannot simply lean on one or even two points of view to guide them in their decisions and actions. That is dangerous and our current times are providing all the evidence for that.

For instance, people are constantly screaming at each other at demonstrations, at debates, and of course, online through the many social media networks at their disposal. People hide behind signs, pseudonyms, or internet identity icons and scream out their views at their perceived adversaries. And they have generally never met each other—heart to heart.

In the circle, people cannot do that. They must be present. They reveal their authentic selves. They become vulnerable. They get an opportunity to truly examine their heart and see what lies there. They begin to know themselves in a different way. And by knowing oneself, a person is ready to learn about another.

Take this idea and place it into schools as open environments. Call them adult learning places if you wish or give them another attractive name, but people must come together and sit down together, and talk openly together about what matters to them, without fear of judgment or reprisal. For teachers, school leaders, and students in such a school that opens its doors, there are additional opportunities to engage new communities of people. There are opportunities to challenge the stereotypes and discriminatory attitudes that are ever-present and ready to strike in any community. There are opportunities to disrupt and challenge views and actions that are harmful to communities.

But getting people there and into a circle is the first step. I can think of many authors who have thought about and written extensively about such actions. Carolyn Shields (2004) comes to mind with her work on diverse communities and communities of difference. She encourages educators and leaders to grow their dialogical leadership competencies. They must be present with their students within mutually benefiting conversations about important topics.

3. Build Collective Leadership; Empower the Students Existing on the Fringes

In 2015, a sixteen-year-old high school new Canadian student went to his English teacher and asked if he could provide his leadership for the incoming group of Syrian students that the school was expecting to welcome and enroll. He had been at the school for nearly a year and was finally getting a grasp on the English language.

The student was steadily immersing himself into the large and active school culture, playing noon-hour sports in the gymnasium and helping the physical education teachers with organizing some of the extracurricular events for the student body. The student had a global mindset, but he still existed on the fringes of the school, because he had come from away and did not truly fit into the general Canadian student culture. His story is inspiring.

He had been born in Iraq in 1998. When the country was ripped open in 2002, his family fled to Syria, a safe country at that time. There he studied through his early grades, but he never really fit into the general Syrian student culture. He was from away. When the Syrian civil war began in 2011, he and his family found themselves, once again, smack in the danger zone. He later told a researcher, "If you want to look at the Middle East, even right now it's like a hunger game. Imagine it like that, a hunger game. Anytime you can die. No . . . no safety guaranteed."

So, the student worked hard, and he learned English; he comprehended how the school worked, and he strived to be a leader in his new Canadian school, in his new Canadian community. He had been through and survived two wars by the time he was fourteen, and he knew what the Syrian students and their families were going through to get safely to Canada. He knew the conflict that they were in and the trauma that many would be wrestling with upon arrival in Canada and long afterward.

He remembered what it was like to sit in the cafeteria and wonder what his Canadian peers were saying in English. He felt lonely and isolated in the language barrier. He did not want that for the new Canadian Syrian students. So, he stepped up without being asked. Without fuss or fanfare. He told a researcher one afternoon, "I went to my teacher and said, 'listen, I know there are more newcomers coming cause it's a new term. If you do not mind, I would like to take them and show them around.'" Being from away, from far away, from worlds away, was not going to stop his leadership. He was not going to exist on the fringes anymore.

Find the Leadership in Your School and Activate It

After so many horrific wars the past twenty to thirty years, humans in countries where military war is absent have witnessed the mass migration of populations flee their homelands, millions live in and work to survive overcrowded refugee camps, and thousands arrive in their communities, like the sixteen-year-old student, to get another chance at life. School leaders, teachers, school counselors, support staff, and the student body are often the first to notice these rapid changes because the parents (or relatives of the dead parents) bring the trauma-filled children to schools to learn. To begin again.

In a high school setting, like the one in the vignette, students are older of course, and have extensive comprehension of what they have been through and the conditions they have survived before making it to the United States, Europe, Australia, New Zealand, or Canada. The leadership capacities that they have developed based on their experiences, far exceed what most North American students have ever undertaken in their lives at the same age.

In this author's work, he has learned the stories of young girls and boys getting their siblings out of their homes before all hell breaks loose. He has learned about young adults raising their younger brothers and sisters in shipping containers in deserts or in stagnant, hot tents in refugee camps. He has learned about so many children going years without any formal education. In fact, two young, female African students who had lived a long time in a refugee camp told him that when they were faced with a choice of using their money to pay for school or for food, they chose education. They chose education. For them, education symbolized better, hope, and freedom.

These students are leaders, and they exist in North American schools that have welcomed (or unfortunately, not welcomed) new immigrants into their learning communities. School leaders, teachers, and students need to find them, empower them, help them build their confidence, and get them away from the margins and fringes of the school culture so they can contribute to the collective growth. It never happens by accident.

That bears repeating. Finding leaders never happens by accident. It is critical that intentionality is part of the collective mindset of the learning community. When new kids come in, get them involved. Sit down and talk with them. Include them and find out what they like to do outside of the curriculum. This is old news, but stories like the one told by the student from Syria are still common.

New immigrant students come in. They do not speak the language; they eat different foods; they wear different clothes. To hell with all of that. They do not have any power and they need to be empowered. They need to belong, and they need support to belong. Here is another story.

You Teach Me, I Teach You, We Teach Together

The high school physical education teacher had a student from India who was learning to speak English. He knew that the student was a regular in the gym at lunchtime on days when the gym was open for students to play a variety of sports. On one day, there were several international and new immigrant students playing a pick-up game of cricket, and the teacher saw how skilled the Indian student was at the game.

The teacher had some money in his P. E. budget. He went online, priced out, and purchased a cricket set. He approached the student and asked him if he would be interested in teaching him how the sport was played, the rules, and some of the nuanced skills he had learned when he was younger. "I don't understand how to play cricket. I've watched it, I don't understand it. I would like you to teach me," The teacher told the student. They agreed.

So, they met for a week in the gym; the student showed his teacher how to do this, that, and the other, and taught him the rules of the game. During that time, the student gained additional vocabulary as he worked with his teacher. The teacher began to understand the game. Their relationship became sealed. Then he told the student, "Good, now we're going to teach other kids how to play."

They played during phys ed class and the student took the lead with his teacher's support. They then started a cricket club at lunch time. Students from Nepal, India, and Pakistan came down. They knew how to play the game. And then, Canadian-born students came in because they had watched the participants having fun and were curious about the game and they started getting involved.

The Indian student took his time and communicated as best he could. The participants carefully listened and followed his instructions. With the support of his teacher, who had empowered him, he started to teach the Canadian students how to play the sport of cricket with the international students.

Have You Read Any Paulo Freire?

That is what the researcher asked the phys ed teacher after learning about the Indian student and the cricket story. The teacher had not read any Paulo Freire and did not really understand, at least in an academic sense, that the dialogue he was intentionally developing with the student was "an existential necessity" (1970; 2005 reprint, p. 88) to help shape the student's confidence, competence, and authentic identity. He brought the student intentionally out of the shadows of his classroom and encouraged him to use his leadership skills.

It was empowering for the student and for the teacher. If there is a dominant theme in Freire's classic book, it is that the teacher cannot be the only teacher in an educative situation. She, he, or they cannot be the only leader and if such instruction and pedagogy is at the heart of a teacher's service, then they are only depositing the content, not engaging the student in any meaningful way, and thus not really helping them transform their life.

The phys ed teacher's work was transformative (Shields, 2018). He didn't know how to even communicate or articulate to the student what it was that he was trying to bring out of him; he was working from his heart knowing that the student would only rise to a certain level without his intervention. Without his encouragement, without intentionality, the student would have just floated through his school experience. What do you think that experience has done for the student's life or for any marginalized student's life?

Leaders, teachers, and even students from all the cultures in the world, you must intentionally look for the leadership on the fringes in your schools and activate it. Otherwise, it is lost forever. And if you are part of a school culture that has this already going on, mentoring supports groups in place, welcoming committees for newcomer students, student and educator intervention teams, then let this part of the book only serve to confirm the great work you are all doing.

4. Engage ALL Communities or Else Suffer the Consequences

Rapid demographic change, technological change, communication complexities, and a multitude of other confounding circumstances have school leaders and educators perpetually scrambling from one fire to the next in their schools and across their communities. They should all wear helmets. But in this writer's mind, the key thing that has been tossed out with the bath water has been effective communication. Without effective communication, there is little chance of relational growth among people. And in our schools, that just does not cut it in 2020 and beyond. People have to engage with each other.

Yes, this part is connected to the first suggestion in this chapter, and the second, and even the third, but it is different enough that it needs some extrapolation. Again, please be patient dear reader.

Like the young administrator in chapter three who learned how to use email in 1999, email also became (as still is) a slight evil in the way it was and continues to be used. Many schools rely on email for their main communication tool; many now rely on school web pages and sending text messaging to parents. In fact, research in this writer's domain has found some schools still sending letters home in one language. Yes, in one language expecting the letter to be read and understood by the adults in the child's home.

Oh dear, what happens if that parent or adult does not speak or even understand that language? What happens if they cannot find someone, like a friend, to interpret and translate the letter for them?

Several years ago, a school secretary was approached by a new immigrant parent who, through his broken English and accent, asked why he had to send his Grade 8 daughter two hours away to a large city to continue her education. The secretary did not know how to respond, and the gentleman was near tears. She called the administrator and together they discovered that the daughter had taken a field trip form home for her parents to sign if they agreed that the child could attend the trip.

The parent understood it to be a transfer letter for his daughter and could only read the name of the city on the form. Being new to the country and unable to understand the historical systems and institutions in place in his new society, in addition to having limited voice and social capital, he thought the school could move his daughter at will.

The administrator and secretary awkwardly explained the process involving a field trip and told him they needed his signature for his daughter to enjoy the trip, and reassured him that she would be home safely that same day, and at a specific hour. They all had a giggle. But it begs the question, why did this have to happen in the first place? With all the technological gadgetry at human disposal, why are these mistakes still being made?

Speaking to teachers in another research project, this author learned of translation devices that were being used in the school by teachers and new immigrant students, but they still were only marginally effective. Communication takes time and too many school leaders and educators do not take the time to communicate effectively. Many say they do not have time.

That may be the case but if you do not communicate effectively all the time, with everyone (and as authentically as you are able to), then you will run into the red zone of despair.

It is time for one last case study. And yes, it is taken verbatim from this professor's toolkit in one of his graduate courses. I hope you enjoy it.

An Educational Reflective Digression

We began a breakfast and lunch program at our school with the help of many people, as well as partnering agencies and community stakeholders in our community. We soon discovered that it does not take long for children to learn that there is food in the school to which they have access.

This program, as important and needed as it was, was at times very challenging to administrate as all our staff wanted children to get what they needed, as delicately as possible without embarrassing children and families, and still, we couldn't afford to have the program taken advantage of in fear of losing our support from contributing stakeholders. This is where school leaders, teachers, and even parent leaders knowing all their families and background realities became critical for our team. Otherwise, considering our experience, we often got trapped in our assumptions and in the unfortunate stereotypes that we sometimes forgot to investigate more closely when distributing the food.

Briefly, here is one such situation we failed to investigate . . . one young lad was asking his teacher for a lunch several times each week, holding his tummy and really constructing a convincible drama. The teacher had a heart of gold and was providing the lunch unconditionally and quietly, every time the child asked for one, and the child was thankful.

Well, one day I came down to my office, after walking through all the classes at lunch, whistling away and reflecting about our successful lunch program, and I was greeted by two very angry parents standing at my office with a lunch bag of food for their child and in another larger bag of what, I did not know at that moment. They had their son, who was in high school and spoke English fairly well, with them.

Through the interpretative skills of their son, the parents demanded that their other son in our school be sent down to the office and they demanded that we go into my office. As you might expect, my heart was racing at 260 beats per minute. I got a little dizzy with fear.

When the boy arrived, I studied his demeanor to gain some sense of what I/we had done and it was evident the lad knew where this was going the minute he saw his parents and older brother and the brown bag his mom was carrying. I invited the parents to sit down, the dad closed my door and the mom proceeded to dump some sandwiches, several bruised pieces of fruit, and some granola bars on my office floor. I was lucky they had taken the old carpet out of my office and replaced it with commercial linoleum because one orange was so rotted, that it absolutely exploded when it hit my floor. I honestly did not know what to think. Did I mention that I was scared?

The father looked up and said, through his Grade 10 son, "Mr. Henry, he (the younger son) has been hiding the food our mom has prepared for him every morning, under his bed. Mr. Henry, we can afford to feed ourselves. Mr. Henry, this is embarrassing for my mom and dad." I stood there shaking and nodding my head in agreement knowing that I was getting my butt kicked and deservingly so. I said sorry many times over and over.

After I explained the whole story and about the support, we were providing children who required food or extra food to build up their lunches, the mom and dad had no disagreement with the program for the children. In my discussion with them and their son that day, I was reminded that as an educator and leader, I must not only espouse the value of getting to know the families whom I/we serve, but I must act in doing so.

As an educator and educational leader, I must adhere to Walker and Dimmock's (2005) proposition and insist that myself and my colleagues not only demonstrate a willingness to understand the cultures and background realities of their students and school communities but support them any way I can in taking those actions. That is one of the moral (Hodgkinson, 1991) and demographic (Banks et al, 2005) imperatives of teaching in complex, diverse schools in today's turbulent world.

The Job Is Communication and Relationship

No one likes getting their butt kicked when they are in a leadership position or leadership role, but it happens quite often and often it is due to factors within the control and wheelhouse of the leader. For sure, everyone overlooks things at some point in their personal or work life; that is excusable. That is forgivable. But when the pace of change is rapid, and there are all types of moving parts that make up the social realities of leaders, teachers, and students in 2020, people must intentionally slow things down or sadly, they will break down. Too many leaders and educators have said, "It is easy for me to tell my colleagues to slow down, it's just that I can't seem to tell myself that." And so, they burn out far too early in their careers. Some change jobs; some play their career out. Digression again. There is so much to cover here.

The school leader had the right intentions, but good intentions are not enough (Shields, 2003). In this case, he needed to get his communication out, and know clearly that it was getting out and, into the minds of all the parents in the school community, most importantly the parents who did not speak the dominant language or hold much cultural capital in the English world. But stretch this idea further. How many other parents from diverse backgrounds do not feel included in the school's community mandate? A leader has got to find this out.

Often the only way is to intentionally engage each family that are part of the school and understand their reality. Get into the communities if you can, and in person. Let community members know who you are, and what the school you lead, or teach at, is about. Make sure they feel welcome and do what you can to get them into the building.

THIS IS NOT ALL

But for now, it will be enough. There are so many things that teachers, school leaders, and students can do in their schools in 2020 and beyond that will contribute to building a better future. A better world. A safer world. Teachers and school leaders must listen to their students. Students must have courage to tell their teachers what their lessons are doing, just as Jen did with Mr. Hernandez. She needed to be filled with hope in her world. That is a great place for education to begin again.

CHAPTER 5 ACTIVITIES AND QUESTIONS

1. Set up a debate in your class related to the use of cell phones.
2. In your school, what sources of engagement activities are there for students, and what is the percentage of the student population participating in them? Do the activities in your school include everyone? Who is not included? Why?
3. What does student leadership mean? There is limited educational research on the subject. Research and write a paper about the many forms that student leadership can take in a kindergarten to Grade 12 school.
4. What do your school leaders and colleagues do to ensure that all families in your school community are included in your learning community?

REFERENCES

Aitken, M. (2017). *The cyber effect.* New York: Spiegel & Grau.
Attenborough, D. (2020). *A life on our planet: My witness statement and a vision for the future.* New York: Grand Central Publishing.

Banks, J. A., Cochran-Smith, M., Moll, L., Richert, A., Zeichnerk, K., LePage, P., et al. (2005). Teaching diverse learners. In L. Darling-Hammond and J. Bransford (Eds.), *Preparing teachers for a changing world: What teachers should learn and be able to do.* San Francisco: Jossey Bass.

Biesta, G. J. and Burbules, N. C. (2003). *Pragmatism and educational research.* Lanham, MD: Rowman & Littlefield.

Brock, E. [1990] (n.d.). "Five ways to kill a man." Retrieved from https://poetryarchive.org/poem/five-ways-kill-man/.

Freire, P. (1970). *Pedagogy of the oppressed.* New York: Continuum.

Hamm, L., Massfeller, H., McLoughlin, J., Bragdon, M., & Hamm, L. A. (2020, October 28). *Expect nothing; appreciate everything: The impact and implications of immigration, demographic changes and increasing diversity on teachers, administrators and students in a New Brunswick high school context – Final Report.* Unpublished monograph. https://unbscholar.lib.unb.ca/islandora/object/unbscholar%3A10278.

Hodgkinson, C. (1991). *Educational leadership: The moral art.* Albany: SUNY Press.

King, S. (2010). *On writing: A memoir of the craft.* New York: Scribner.

LensShift. (2018). Six/Nine: Matter of perspective cartoon. Retrieved from https://www.lensshift.org/library/six-nine-matter-of-perspective-cartoon.

Orlowski, J. (2020). *The social dilemma* [film]. Netflix.

Palmer, P. (2007). *The courage to teach: Exploring the inner landscape of a teacher's life.* San Francisco, CA: Jossey-Bass.

Shields, C. (2003). *Good intentions are not enough: Transformative leadership for communities of difference.* Lanham, MD: Scarecrow Press.

Shields, C. M. (2004). Dialogic leadership for social justice: Overcoming pathologies of silence. *Educational* administration quarterly, *40*(1), 109–132.

Shields, C. M. (2018). *Transformative leadership in education: equitable changes in an uncertain and complex world (second edition).* New York: Routledge.

The Tragically Hip. (1996). Springtime in Vienna [Recorded by The Tragically Hip]. *Trouble at the henhouse* [Alternative Rock]. Bath, Ontario: MCA.

Walker, A. and Dimmock, C. (2005). Leading the multiethnic school: Research evidence on successful practice. *The educational forum, 69,* 291–304.

Chapter 6

Why Peace?

Two teams from two different communities, hundreds of miles separating them, were preparing themselves for a championship game. The winner of this series would move on and play the winner from the next region, taking one more step toward a national berth. The players, aged sixteen to twenty-one, were in their respective dressing rooms prior to the warmup listening to music and adjusting their protective equipment so they did not have to worry about how it felt during the game. The music stopped playing and the buzz of the large crowd entering the stadium could be heard.

The players were all bred from birth to play this game. This beautiful, flowing, artful, violent game. The previous year, thousands of miles away from this event, a Korean passenger jet had caressed Soviet airspace and without warning, was destroyed in a flash by a missile from a Soviet fighter pilot. Hundreds of lives were lost in that moment. The disaster had brought the Cold War to its very height and placed the entire world on the brink of a *WarGames* confrontation. This time, it was for real. There would be no savvy Hollywood actors brave and smart enough to hack into a nation's computer system and stop the madness, put an end to the turbulence. It was life imitating art.

But on this night as the players yelled their battle cries and raced out onto their stage, they were only thinking of one thing. To hurt, to punish, to destroy. To win. They were not interested in politics, in global events, or in any of the wars that were going on around the world. It was 1984, and they did not have immediate access to conflicts. There were no cell phones; there was no social media. They did not type or text. They still wrote in cursive. But they all understood hatred. They were bred by their coaches, their parents, their teammates, to do so.

The teams moved around on their respective sides, stretching, and flexing their muscles. The players looked blankly at their opponents on the other side. The sound of the crowd, the loud music in the stadium, the smell of the food being sold made everything blurry. Their bodies took them through warmup; they did not have to think about what they were doing.

But two players, one white, one with darker skin, on either side of the center line, made eye contact. Neither wanted to look away first. They stared at each other as their teammates warmed up around them on their side. They sneered. Their teeth clenched and their nostrils flared. Their teammates, a mixture of races, languages, religious beliefs, skin colors were oblivious to the imminent flash point about to happen. The two moved aggressively toward each other and one foot crossed over the center line.

"Get the fuck on your side, you jerk!"

"I am on my side, you prick!"

They shoved each other back and forth over the line. They hated each other. They had seen each other numerous times over their lives on this same type of battlefield. One wore one color; one wore another. In the moment, they hated each other. They wanted to hurt each other. Their teammates smelled the hatred and turned toward the centerline. The crowd saw this happening and began to scream and encourage them. The flash point was going to happen.

"Fuck off!"

"You fuck off!"

And their fists came higher into each other's face. They knew each other; they had seen each other time and time again on the battlefield.

"I am going to kill you tonight!"

"I am going to knock your teeth out!"

And they came together full force with all their power, and they swung at each other and made contact. And there was blood and pain and violence. And then their teammates joined at the line, and over it, and the violence escalated. And the fans in the stadium were screaming from the side to kill each other. And the two young men in the center of it all kept swinging at each other, their eyes wide open with hatred, not feeling the pain, not caring how much they hurt and were hurt. It was 1984. Life was mirroring art.

And then they tired, and the energy of the violence melted away. And the two players looked at each and saw the blood flowing from each other's nose, mouth. They did not see their teammates fighting. They did not hear the crowd. They did not feel the blood streaming down their face. They looked into each other's eye and felt sorry—empathy. They knew how the other felt.

And then there was a calm and players returned to their side and the two players looked at each other bewildered, now knowing each other's strength. Now they knew each other in another way, but not in a good way. There was respect. There was shame. Only later, much later, would there be wisdom and forgiveness.

And that was the problem. They had never talked about fishing, or mysteries, or their fears, or about their dreams and their families with each other. They did not know each other. They only knew each other in the arena, on a stage. They did not give themselves an opportunity to understand each other outside of the competition they both loved and participated in, and that is a problem. Why does wisdom and forgiveness come so late in life?

IN MY CRAFT OR SULLEN ART—THOMAS

Leaders lead, teachers teach, students learn. And the cycle continues. Politicians persuade, protesters march, and large corporations keep getting richer. And the cycle continues. Inequities increase, raw resources are harvested and manufactured into consumer goods, and finally, society is crippled by a global pandemic. The cycle is finally broken. There is a pause. There is finally a slowness, a calm. Then the cycle begins again.

And there is more, lots more to pour into our current social reality that will cause much despair, much hopelessness, in 2020. But it is now 2021. This year, this entire year has blurred all realities and it needs to end. It will finally end. The turbulence of this historic, complex, terrifying year will end and by the time the book is in the hands of readers, perhaps, just perhaps the world will be back on a gentler course, if humans have gained a little wisdom about the events they have endured together.

If anything, the total social chaos of 2020 is nothing more than a snapshot and this author has only attempted to capture some of it. That is all. COVID-19 did not dominate. It will not dominate.

Dylan Thomas wrote that writers should write because they enjoy their craft. Not for "ambition or bread or the strut and trade of charms on the ivory stages." Writing is a sullen art mostly performed in isolation, in a writer's creative environment. Watching, thinking, writing is a human act and sometimes a simple idea can grow legs (or get wings which is better) and connect with other ideas, forge new ideas, and possibly nourish a new way of thinking, acting and effectively responding to the complexities in one's life and social spaces, bringing humanity closer together.

A friend once reminded the author that in research activities involving leadership, teaching, and learning, "Our task is not to see what no one else has seen, but to think that which no one else has thought, about that which everyone sees" (Schopenhauer, n.d.). To use the overused cliché once again, humans cannot be doing the same things in the world and expect better and different results. At the end of 2021, that idea rings loudly.

People cannot be standing across a line from each other sneering, pushing, and punching either physically or psychologically. It is time for the lines to disappear and for people to come together, respect each other's races, spaces, and ideas about sharing the limited resources left on the planet. More importantly, how to sustain those resources and not further destroy them. Perhaps that is hoping for too much. Still, keep hoping. Continue to hope. Keep hope alive.

This author has not been the first to write about cruelty, suffering, disease, and turbulence in the world, and he certainly won't be the last, as the next few decades look to be very much like the scene that opens this final chapter if in fact some serious change does not occur. The players on the stage are from a specific sport and they are from many sports.

The players in the scene are from a specific industry and they are from many industries. The players in the scene are from a specific community, and they are from many communities. The players in the scene are from a specific protest movement and they are from many such movements. The players in the scene are from a specific school, and sadly, they are from many schools.

Such behavior as this writer chose to describe to push the book to its eventual closure is everywhere in the world, on every platform, and in every tool that humans have accessible to them in 2021. Confronting it all seems daunting, but confronting it, is what every person, every leader, teacher, and student needs to do. And in the previous chapter, four strategies were posited and briefly developed, though this writer was not the first to write about each. It is simply what he believes is important for schools and the people within them to strongly consider as they all move together forward and hopefully together with a collective spirit.

Yet, there is one thing that this world needs more of and now more of it than ever, and it is peace and an authentic commitment to achieving a common social harmony. That is going to be the ultimate test for ALL humans in the next while because there is just so much discontent, disinformation, and social disillusion that cause so many people just to give up. Many just simply give up.

Instead of thinking and working together, they join this fight and that fight, this protest movement and that one, screaming and swearing at each other with their heavenly or hellish cause and, here's the clincher . . . they are getting nowhere. Violence only begets violence as the opening scene clearly illustrated. And that scene is being played out everywhere in 2021.

People are falling victim to their ideology of the moment, whatever they choose to believe and follow, and sadly, learning to hate even more. There does not seem to be much forgiveness in this current world so people will go on living within the boundaries and sins of the history they know, or do not know that well. They believe what someone tells them, what they read in the news they choose to read, on the channels they choose to watch. They do not want the full picture, because the full picture will make them think more.

And whether people are right or wrong in 2021, once their current fights end, they most likely will pick up with another cause because hating for them is easier than loving, easier for them than forgiving, than saying sorry. Many just cannot say, I am wrong, also. It is through hate that too many people find their courage and voices. It is in 2021, with all the technological consumer devices at hand, that give them the digital streets and avenues to express their hatred and unkindness. It is their hatred that is extinguishing peace efforts. And if you get rid of one group of political leaders, you will get another set, and the bureaucratic machine will keep humming and running, and not much will change in an ocean of hatred in which nearly eight billion people are treading. This MUST end.

A single theory will not guide or show people, particularly those who work with children in highly diverse educational contexts and communities, as parts of this book outlined, the way through and way out of the hatred. This is a time for blending theories in schools (Rayner, 2009) on imaginative pathways that no one has thought much on through the depleted and broken-limbed forests of the world; only then can new ideas emerge from the ashes of 2020 and the last twenty years that this book has predominantly addressed. In peace and through peace is the only way forward. The madness must stop.

WHY PEACE IN 2021?

The question seems explanatory in a response. If it were, then surely society would have achieved some level of equilibrium or some utopian bliss. And society has not. Our social world is fraught with peacelessness, sleeplessness, and extensive anxiety in fact. It is civil discontent on the abyss of civil war and the world is one major flash point away from total social disaster. School leaders, educators, and students, you MUST learn about peace and embrace it.

You MUST find and establish a common definition that includes everyone regardless of their background, physical or emotional appearance, and the ways they choose to see and understand their world in which they belong. Difference is the new buzzword, and you MUST learn to live it and love it. Otherwise, you get what you get and if you look around, you will see what that is. That is, conflict, chaos, and turbulence with no end.

The thing about peace is that it is common, we all see it, know what it is, and to some degree, even live it. But as Schopenhauer suggests, humans must look at it differently to understand it better. Peace begins with a simple smile. Yet it cannot be a Claudius-type smile of deceit and manipulation (from Shakespeare's *Hamlet*), just a genuine smile. A genuine and simple recognition of the human being you are walking past by voluntarily exercising the muscles in your cheeks slightly and showing some of your teeth. A smile. It costs nothing.

Kindness costs nothing. And, it is easier to do if you do not have your head down, eyes on your phone as you are walking somewhere. Pay attention to the people in your social world and acknowledge them with an expression of openness and nonviolence, and then the thorny pathway to acceptance and understanding begins to germinate. That is hard to do if you are carrying a sign of some type at a social or political demonstration where you take your discontent, anger, and frustration and shove it all in someone's face. Like the two players did in the opening story.

Or worse yet, you take all of that and do the same on some digital platform. Remember, you are, we all are, one flash point away from a major social disruption. As the players learned in the opening, you cannot fight your way to peace. You cannot fight your way to victory. You just cannot. It is an illusion. Everyone loses because a fight never ends; it only takes a pause and then looks for another opportunity to start. Look through sport; look through politics; look through history.

But enough of that philosophizing, this last argument is about schools everywhere and if they do not have a peace plan in place in 2021, then the question is, where are the leaders and educators really taking ALL their students? Yes, ALL is capitalized because all the students must be encouraged and brought on board. There must be all-hands-on-deck for peace. Because students are not going to the same place the way education is currently structured in 2021.

The stronger and richer students will continue to get more opportunities; the less fortunate, fewer opportunities. Fighting has not changed that, but perhaps peace just might. Think about peace differently. Can you think about it as a common, collective, organized peace?

Humans must think about this in a different way. Why does peace matter? What does peace mean in a school? What types of discussions involve peace? Deep-seated peace? What types of learning situations grow peace among children, colleagues, the community? Is peace in the vision statement on the wall along with all the latest educative phrases? Is it there? Because if it is not, then peace is not at the core of the learning and social program in the school. And, that is dangerous in a delicate, diverse society that is constantly a flash point away from a disaster.

All the Way Back to Desmond Doss

Peace is about social justice, but quite often, social justice is not about peace. The social justice warriors of today are fighting from all sides (yes, they are on all sides) from all political and theoretical persuasions. They are noisy, they are everywhere, and they cluster up the conversations. They do not practice peace. People fighting for social justice often use violence or become violent when engaged by an opposing force that just might view social justice in a different way.

This author loves and believes in social justice and equity and has his own struggles and professional agenda for social justice in place. Yet, he has come to understand that without peace, there can be no social justice. There can be no discussion, conversation, friendly encounter, dialogue. And "dialogue cannot exist without humanity" (Freire, 1970, p. 90). That has been a defining moment in his career. Without peace, there can be no social justice. There can be no social justice without peace. This is about peace, peace, peace. It must be first.

As the character of Desmond Doss brilliantly illustrated in the movie *Hacksaw Ridge*, "With the world so set on tearing itself apart, it doesn't seem so bad to me to want to put a little bit of it back together." That is our world. That is our children's world, now in 2021. School leaders, educators, and students, if you want to lead, then lead. If you want to teach, then teach. If you want to learn, then keep learning. But do it all through peace.

How does one go about building peace in a world that is on fire? What does that look like in an educational setting? Can an education plan become a peace plan? Can the three-year school improvement plan be an education and peace plan? If so, what would school leaders, teachers, and students think about and write down in such a plan to guide them through the year? The next three years? It must be written down and yes, students, too are part of the peace process. They must be the thinkers and authors of the peace plan with the educators. They cannot be left out.

Remember, students are going to be the teachers, leaders, and stewards of the world shortly, if not now. They cannot be told what they need to do about peace; they must be fully engaged and in on the conversation, right from preschool to the end of school. Yes, get those children who are just learning to talk in sentences, tie their shoes, and learning their numbers and colors, to be agents of peace. Educators must do everything they can with the time they have with them to not send them to the next year with any hatred-residue in their hearts. It is too dangerous; 2021 needs agents of peace.

AGENTS OF PEACE IN 2021 AND BEYOND

What do agents of peace look like? What do they think about? How do they act? Start with protection, but in the nonviolent strain. Protection of the ground, protection of the water, protection of built structures. Peace agents must think about these things and why they are valuable and necessary and why bringing harm to them is bringing harm unto self and others.

How can they do this without signs and protests? That is a great problem to figure out. So, figure it out. You know that protests and signs and social media magnification will only raise suspicion, distrust, and stall communication toward any progress for peace. Figure it out. This author is not going to tell you what he would do, because you might not do that or even be able to do that.

But getting to know who is hurting the ground, the water, and the human-built structures is probably the first step. Remember, you are an agent of peace. You do not have sports equipment, a gun, or a microphone; you only have your mind and your courage.

Restore things, pick things up, and take care of things. Let other people understand why caring for things is important. Do not walk past garbage. Pick it up and place it where it needs to go. Learn how to work with plastics and how to discard them appropriately. Humans can reduce their use, but plastics are going to be with humans for a great deal longer. They cannot just go into the ground or water.

Leaders, teachers, students, try to figure it out in your schools and communities. You can do it. One young woman just received international recognition for her environmental advocacy in Canada. It is an inspiring story and demonstrates the power of peace and what student leadership can be and can accomplish (d'Entremont, 2020). It is like the young man who knew what the Syrian students would encounter once they were in his school and he decided to do something about it. Peace does not stand on the sidelines.

Peace is mentoring. School leaders, educators, and students must understand that human connection does not happen without intentional actions. If it happens accidently, it rarely lasts. Without people standing up to help and supporting other people, there can be no peace. That is why mentoring in all the iterations can be a crucial moment for human growth. Peace groups, mentoring groups, welcoming teams must all be written into the education and peace plan along with all the strategies that take most of the space for academic growth.

Is it more important for students to be able to exist in peace in their world, contribute to a peaceful world, build a peaceful world, or get a better English grade? Does getting a better English grade help them become resilient? Or does kindness, feeling a sense of belonging, and friendship help them become resilient? Priorities are really screwed up in education in 2021.

Are we preparing children to simply be part of this complex, consumer-inducing technological world or are we preparing children to take care of each other and the earth? Can you do both? It is unlikely in 2021.

SING THRUSH, SING!

It is time to end this book and perhaps begin another. The final lesson for 2020 is at hand. It is December 31st. The world is heading into some more dark months. People must work harder to avoid dark spaces and dead spots ahead of them. People can do this if they stand together. Hope will return. Like Frodo who did not ask for all the burdens that the ring brought him, humans who survived 2020 and 2021 must bear some more darkness before the light returns.

The poet Thomas Hardy wrote a wonderful poem at the end of the nineteenth century called "The Darkling Thrush." In it, the speaker says he is "fervouslous" as he describes a desolate landscape extending from his bleak and defeated mindset.

All of a sudden, from above the speaker's head, "An aged thrush, frail, gaunt, and small / In blast-beruffled plume / Had chosen thus to fling his soul / Upon the growing gloom." The sound of the bird's song was enough to wrestle the speaker out of his woeful, depressive slumber. There was in that moment "Some blessed Hope, whereof he knew / And I was unaware."

English teachers would be well encouraged to teach this poem and relate its setting and theme to the end of 2020 and perhaps 2021. The ray of light that is breaking through each day is the light and hope that students, teachers, and school leaders need in their schools. They need each other in human terms, face to face, and that message is loud and clear. All the technology humans have access to cannot replace the importance of human to human contact in a common educational setting. The screen is not the answer. People cannot lead, teach, and learn online all the time. It just does not work. Sing aged thrush, sing.

CHAPTER 6 ACTIVITIES AND QUESTIONS

1. Does the opening vignette mirror what is happening in the social world today? Please explain.
2. What does peace mean? What does peace look like to you?

3. Does your school or organization have a peace plan in place? Why or why not?
4. Teaching students about peace and how to grow peace in their worlds enables them to become academically and socially competent. Do you agree or disagree with this statement? Explain your view.

REFERENCES

d'Entremont, D. (2020). Nova Scotia teen wins international award for river cleanup work. *CBC.* Retrieved from https://www.cbc.ca/news/canada/nova-scotia/nova-scotia-teen-wins-international-award-for-river-cleanup-work-1.4776331.

Hardy, T. (1900). "The darkling thrush." Retrieved from https://www.poetryfoundation.org/poems/44325/the-darkling-thrush.

Rayner, S. (2009). Educational diversity and learning leadership: A proposition, some principles and a model of inclusive leadership. *Educational review, 61*(4), 433–447.

Schopenhauer, A. (n.d.). Retrieved from https://www.goodreads.com/author/quotes/11682.Arthur_Schopenhauer.

About the Author

Lyle "Steamer" Hamm is an associate professor of educational administration and leadership in the faculty of education at the University of New Brunswick in Fredericton. His teaching and scholarship focus on social action theory, teaching, and leadership in demographically changing schools and communities. He is also interested in and has written about intercultural citizenship education, peace building, and how to improve school culture and climate through mentoring and coaching practices. Lyle served as an educator and administrator in Alberta for twenty-two years before he joined UNB in 2013. He can be reached at lhamm@unb.ca or via his office phone at (506) 447-3152.

Manufactured by Amazon.ca
Bolton, ON

21710433R00076